How to Day Trade Forex for High Profits

Tips to make High Profits Trading Forex

By Joe Corrado

Copyright 2016

Why you should read this entire book

There are a lot of pre-education and pre-trading decisions you will need to make *before* you spend any money on trading or capitalizing an account to trade live with as a brand new self-directed trader. **How to Day Trade Forex for High Profits** delivers a *basic* comprehensive guide to some of the intermediate tools and resources needed to help give you the best beginner information to make some of those hardest decisions and also gives you some intimidate principles to help you begin making high profits right away from your investing and trading business.

Almost all the professional investors and traders I know do not even worry about the making money. They are much more concerned on managing their capital and risk in the live markets. It's really not about making money it is about *keeping* the capital you *already* have. There is some review in this book on money management and a few other things that you may have already read, not to worry because learning trading well enough to actually make an income from it will require you to do things over and over and over again until they are first nature to you.

The reason you bought **How to Day Trade Forex for High Profits** and why it is unique is that it is going to tell you about the who, what, where, when and how about what you need to know to be able to trade and invest in today's financial markets (or any tradable market) with confidence and zero fear and to be able to do it the right way from the start *on as little as $500 capital to start with.*

To make any of the principles in this book work for you it is *absolutely critical* that you have a handle on the beginner principles I talk about in my book **Beginners Guide to Self-Directed Day Trading.** Everyone has to start somewhere and the information in my first book gives you all of the baseline information you need to start off in this business the right way from the first day.

When you are done reading **How to Day Trade Forex for High Profits** you will have an excellent *basic* explanation of some intermediate techniques that can be used to increase your profits from live trading. The information in this book will put you on the *fast track* to becoming a successful self-directed financial market investor and trader with very little money invested other than the cost of this book.

You should already have made the first decisions as to *what* you want to study and *how* you plan to do your education in order for you to be able to make your own self-directed investment decisions with real money in the live currency, stock or futures markets.

The road to success in investing and trading as I always say is paved with the smoking blown up accounts of investors and traders. It did not have to be a long hard and expensive road though. It can be a road paved with gold and be fairly easy if you just take time to learn this business the right way from the start on your first day, *keep it simple and it will be.*

The *basics* to investing and day trading the live financial markets to make money every day with the smart money *are not that hard* once you have mastered the first few things you need to know which are money management, chart reading and price action and your own trading psychology just name a few. Use the extra clickable links provided at the end of the book to do more of your own research to incorporate some of these principles into your core trading strategy.

Your core strategy *can* and *should* be *very simple* and really all you will need to make money with the smart money every day in the live financial markets or *any* liquid market for that matter. I use the techniques in this book every time I initiate a position in the live market after doing my due diligence and research.

Once you know how to incorporate these techniques into your trading method, you will find they are very practical and can be used in the live financial markets in an intelligent and methodical way every day. When you have it down pat you will have a lethal double whammy method to make as much money as you *want* or *need*. The beauty of it is that it can be used in *all* liquid markets and *all* time frames making it a robust method that is easily repeatable across any asset.

The professional advice I give you in this book will *empower you* to have confidence and zero fear of going in the live markets and accurately initiating a low risk high reward position with which you can have a high probability outcome from being a live market participant. Becoming a successful self-directed investor and trader is not nearly as difficult as one would think as long as they have the proper education and proper knowledge base right from day one, it takes a while but **you can do it**!

I feel **How to Day Trade Forex for High Profits** does an excellent job in explaining the very first things a new investor and trader needs to know *before* even doing anything. It is meant to be a spring board for the very first educational information that a new person needs for a baseline to get started from.

Learning to change bad habits developed by having the wrong information to start off with are *very hard to break*. Listen to what it says to do in **How to Day Trade Forex for High Profits** and *don't develop any bad habits to begin with* and you could be cruising your money train down to the bank everyday consistently.

Another reason you should read this whole book is so that you can avoid the mistakes that 97% of retail sheeple of the herd and retail traders make from day one. All of the books in my brand new investor and trader series talk about those reasons in detail so that you *don't have to waste years* finding it all out the hard way and expensive way on your own. *You're welcome!*

Many of the things I tell brand new investors and traders in all my books may sound like I am a broken record and some things you read may sound repetitive. I do that for a specific reason because much of what trading is about is doing those same actions over and over again repetitively to make money the same way every day. It is the only way professional traders do it and how they develop their edge to win in the live markets against the best market participants in the world. Some of the tips you'll read in **Beginner Day Trader Tip Book** will reinforce information you should have already studied in my other books and are currently using in your investing and trading already.

If you have been learning this business from the ground up then the principles in **How to Day Trade Forex for High Profits** are the next step in helping you to gain that needed edge over your competition. I encourage you to read it *as many times as it takes* for it to become clear to you as to what you need to do to make these techniques work for you to make you the high profits you're looking for in the live markets. Remember there are *no money back guarantees* in the financial markets however you must know the *right* information from the start to have a chance of becoming consistently profitable and financially successful.

Table of Contents

Why you should read this entire book

Have you become a money manager yet?

Are you working with a rule based plan yet?

Your trading method should be what the markets work and that is supply and demand

Having the 3 p's patience, probability and persistence in your favor

Always follow the path of least resistance

3 things that will help you win more trades – large PM, correlation, confluence in signals

How to overcome over trading as a beginner

How to overcome the fear of "pulling the trigger" on a trade

Ways beginners can increase their winning percentage for higher profits

Front running the smart money

What is high probability trading?

How to put the probabilities to make high profits in your favor – using probability boosters

Why you need to always look at the bigger picture

The old buy low and sell high routine

My final advice to new self-directed traders

Extra links

Glossary

Disclaimer

Have you become a money manager yet?

Remember that in this business *no money means no trading* so some review is important at this juncture to reinforce what you should already know that will make you high profits in the live financial markets.

This section is worth its weight in gold and the information is *priceless* for a brand new self-directed trader and while lengthy it is a necessary review and worth every cent you paid for this book. If you have zero experience or have already started your trading business but have begun to falter it's OK. The information I am going to give to you in this section is the *most important information you will ever receive in your trading career about money* so I encourage you to really take the time to absorb it and follow it if you would like to be a consistently profitable market participant.

Strict money management and risk control *is essential* to achieve long-term success in the financial markets. The high level of leverage and margin available to traders makes it important to manage risk exposure and to avoid overleveraged positions. As I said earlier if you are going to use leverage or margin you had better learn *everything* about it and what can happen to you if you get jammed up on a trade going bad on you. *Always trade with a stop loss!*

If I had only 1 tip I could give brand new self-directed investors and traders coming into the business who have zero knowledge and have not done any research, training or education yet, I would tell them to study money management and risk management first *before* they even begin to look at any other information about the investing and trading business. If you only take away one thing from reading this entire book I would tell you it should be that to study money management and risk management *first* will be the most important you have ever done for yourself as an investor and trader.

New people *do not spend nearly enough time* learning about risk management and money management and it gets them into trouble right from the start. You need to have a risk management plan to be able to be consistently profitable in investing and trading in the live markets. If you don't, you mine as well write a check to your broker for the entire balance of your capital account because you will undoubtedly lose *every bit of it* without a plan.

Being wrong in trading isn't *wrong* however *staying wrong* in trading will be *death* to your account! Your job in your investing and trading business is to be a money manager not a money maker. You get paid to take risks yes, however you have to be an expert at controlling them, the money is just a byproduct of that function. The truth of it is simple, money management wins over time, there is no other way to put it. The very first thing that a brand new trader should learn and *understand completely* is risk and money management.

All of the people I know in this business who are money makers actually do not even worry about making money. There sole focus is preserving the capital *they already have*. They manage their risk on every position at all costs and know that they can have a loser every now and then and are ok with it.

When people ask me for help getting started in the trading business one of the first things I ask them is if they have studied money management and risk management. To many times I have had people come to me for mentoring help and I ask them how much time they spent on learning money management. Most of the time, the answer I get is "what do you mean"; it never surprises me and is the response I anticipate.

If a brand new trader takes the time to learn money management in the beginning there won't be any having to go backward in the learning curve, which can get *verrrrry* expensive. Unfortunately *no one* tells new traders they need to study money management first and they are left to fill in the blanks themselves. Well now, if you have purchased this book and you are brand new to trading, you know that you need to study money management first if you don't want to lose money in the live market.

The number one thing I have people learn who come to me for help when they are first starting out is risk and money management, they don't get to learn *anything* else before this is mastered 100%. This is the one area where most new people make some of their mistakes. I find that they are quick to jump into trading their demo accounts once they have some knowledge about the mechanics of trading however they have spent *very little* or *no time at all* on learning money management. Once they start losing money right away they wonder what the heck is happening and *why* things are working like they thought.

Everyone wants to make *some* money in the live markets. That is what this business is all about however one must take the *proper steps* to make sure that they have all of the information to be able to do so in the *live* market. Without proper money management skills it is very easy to develop bad habits on the demo account which when taken with them into a live market situation *can cause serious damage* to a real money account and *very quickly*. These bad habits are very hard to break once they are developed and ingrained into the traders psyche.

In learning money management a new self-directed investor or trader can begin to see what their own personal risk tolerance is. You *must* know this *before* ever stepping foot in the live market with your hard earned real money. There are plenty of scenarios and formulas for risk management however what most investors and traders find out is that they will only want to lose a *set sum of money* before saying OK that's enough and close out a losing position with a loss. Part of being a winning professional trader is to learn how to lose professionally as well. You *will not* win every single position you enter, you should *also* be prepared for *that*.

Money management in the live market is what it is all about not trading. You don't actually make money by trading you make money by being in the market *in* your position. If you don't have any money left you can't *be* in the market.

To succeed at trading the financial markets, you need to not only thoroughly understand position sizing, and risk amount per trade, you also need to *consistently execute* each of these aspects of money management in combination with a highly effective yet simple to understand trading strategy that uses price action in conjunction with supply and demand principles.

Learning money management requires time and attention to detail that most all new self-directed traders are not willing to do. Once you have a live position in the market you go from be a trader to a risk and money manager. The only thing you have control over once you are in the live market is how much money you *don't lose*.

Experienced successful investors and traders know that employing a rule based money management strategy is one of critical concepts of risk management. Money management for account preservation is not sexy at all and very boring to study however they are *the most important* skills in investing and trading that person in the business need to have an understanding of and to have *mastered*.

If you *cannot* fully grasp and understand the implications of money management as well as how to actually implement money management principles and techniques, you have a *very limited* chance of becoming a consistently profitable trader. Until you *completely understand* and *are comfortable with* how to have, and how to follow a money management plan I encourage you to **stay out** of the live market.

Not learning proper trade and money management – Not using stop losses and cutting losses early. You hear that a million times in your investing and trading career. Why is it then, that almost every brand new investor and trader lacks this skill? They have not taken the time to learn this very important skill from the start and it almost always causes them some account pain in the beginning.

The main reason why the professionals are so successful is because they stick to their plan no matter if they are losing money or making a lot of money. They *do not ever* deviate from their plan because they know that over a long period of time they will be consistently profitable from having done so.

Having a set plan and also having it automated so your profit target and stop loss are deployed when your position is executed in the live market is another way to avoid making money mistakes. As I said before, the only thing you have control of once you are in the live market is how much money you *don't lose*. By doing it this way and having it automated you can take out some of the stress involved when your real money is working in the live market.

A money management plan for the type of trading you are doing should be tailored to what *your* risk appetite is *not* anyone else's. Trading is a very personal business and what works for one trader *will not* work for another. Another way to make your money management plan your own is to compose it to what market you are working and also what time frame you are working in that market.

Your plan should take into account the volatility of the market, time of day you are trading, how many lots or contracts you are trading with. Most successful traders in the market have this information incorporated into their plan and that is what makes them so successful.

The first and foremost thing about money management is to have a plan and then <u>*actually* use it</u>. To many times traders will compose a money management plan, go in the live market, get into some trouble on a position and the plan goes *out the window*. Unfortunately so does *large amounts* of their risk capital most of the time.

I tell brand new traders what they will find that works for them the best is the *most simple* money management strategy that they can come up with. They will not know for sure how successful it will be, however that is better than to not have anything in place and doing nothing. The only people I know who make money every day in the markets are the people who have great money management skills, and are well capitalized for the type investing and trading they do. To do it any other way invites financial disaster and risk of ruin. Don't be *that* trader!

Once you have studied risk management and then apply it to how you want to invest and trade you can begin to have some success *as long as* you stick to your money management plan and <u>*never*</u> deviate from it. This is where most retail traders get themselves into trouble and cause themselves to lose money. They will set a stop loss and then when price action approaches the stop they will adjust it or take it out altogether. **BAD IDEA!** Once your stop loss is in the market you should *never move it*.

Risk in investing and trading is *unavoidable* however with the proper training and a good sound plan can be diminished when the plan is followed. Risk is also diminished over time when the investor and trader gains more knowledge as to how much appetite for risk they really have. Without this knowledge the investor or trade cannot gain an understanding or get the experience and competence to make consistent profits.

When you make the decision to go live with real money, that's when it gets serious and very real for you. You are now in competition with the big boys, who have billions of dollars to play with and have the best super computer technology in the world and code slinging geeks to tell the computer what to see and what trades to execute, and they can see you coming a mile away so you *better know WTF* to do.

You absolutely need to have a competitive edge in the markets, and you must have it *before* you do anything in the live markets with real money. If you run with the 'sheeple of the herd' you can be assured to *not have any edge* so don't, they all study the same information and are all programmed the same way to lose money repeatedly.

To be consistently profitable over the long term one must consider capital preservation their number one rule. *To be successful in this business it cannot be any other way.* It takes money to make money in the financial markets and _once your money is gone it is gone_. This is why I tell clients they *must* study risk and money management *first* and *foremost*.

The moment your deploy capital in the live market you go from being an investor or day trader to a risk and money manager. You have *already* determined the probabilities of having a positive outcome on a position before you took it. Now all there is to do is sit back and let the market pay you by managing your risk on the position. Once you have your money management plan and rules in place it is critical that you be disciplined to follow the plan and all the rules at all costs. It is best to have them written out in a word document or a spread sheet and kept right by you at your work station at all times for reference if you need to.

A trick I have traders I help out use is to set their demo account balance to whatever amount they think they will be going to capitalize their real money account with, this way they will know *right off* if they can work in the live market with that amount of capital or not.

I did not choose to do that and the first time I went in the live futures market and as I said, I promptly lost two thousand dollars. I got back out and studied more. I went back in the live market again and lost *another* two thousand dollars. Now I am down a total of four thousand dollars real money and scratching my head going dude WTF.

The reason I had lost some money is because I did not have any money management skills developed. What I just said I lost is the perfect example of that. The live market *is not* the place to be if you have not done your proper education. There are sharks with fully loaded revolvers in the market waiting for you.

Risk management should be very important to you as a trader if you want to be consistently profitable. You always need to be thinking in terms of capital preservation and not worried as much about capital appreciation. If your plan is solid, the money will come on its own if you are following your rule based plan. Your job as a trader is not to make money your job is to *manage* the money you *already have* so you can make more.

Even if you were careless and lost only 50% of your capital you would still need to make 100% to get all your money back. It is possible to do this albeit very hard, and *not likely*, especially for the retail sheeple of the herd. Once they begin to lose money they will start to jump around to different asset classes and systems, this only compounds their problems.

All the trading books (including mine), say that you should not ever risk more than 1 – 2% of available trading capital on any given day trade. On Swing trades, this number may be 3 – 5% of their trading capital. You will have a maximum dollar amount you can lose on any trading day, and *you will cease trading immediately when that number is hit*. What this number is to you depends on your account size. *You should never trade more than you are willing to lose*. The larger your account is *the less* you should be using as risk. On some of my accounts I use .025%.

If you set your daily goal at $600 dollars and are risking $200 on a trade and are stopped out 3 times then *you are done* for that trading day. Turn your charts off and go have a good day. The market will be there waiting for you the next time.

Trading and thinking like a consistently profitable trader will allow your trading to improve enormously and the profits will come much easier as you learn to control your risk and let the profits take care of themselves. Always using a SL that's within your comfort level as far as risk goes. You get paid to take risk. So take risk! But also be a money manager. Everyone I know in this business has the goal of having their SL *as close to their entry* as possible thus having the lowest amount of risk possible. Experienced traders control risk, inexperienced traders just chase money. **You will not have a 100 % success rate**... if you win 51 % and lose 49 % you just need to make a nice living out of the 2 % difference.

The capital one starts their business with should be capital that is *disposable*. Meaning that if all the capital happened to be lost to the markets the investor or trader would not be hurt by the loss *in any way*. I have clients I mentor do visualization; I have them think about throwing their starting capital into their barbeque and turning it on and watching their money burning up in flames and smoke.

It sounds harsh I know, however *the reality of it is* that when a new investor or trader who has entered the business is not using a rules based plan, has not done the proper education and training and learned what they need to know to take only high probability positions that will give the highest reward and have the lowest risk the outcome is virtually almost always the same. Flames and smoke!

There is also plenty of information on risk management and money management online. I would tell you to figure out *what type* of trader you want to be and to figure out what your money goals are first and then tailor your money management plan to the goals you set for yourself. Learn the *right* information the *right way* from the *first* day and you should have *no problems*.

Protecting their capital is what professional trader's do most however they also take great steps to protect the amount of unrealized profit that becomes part of the total equity of his account. To the experienced professional protecting profits is just as important as protecting themselves and limiting losses.

Manage your risk capital with a good risk management profile, and you will be in the markets for as long as you want to be in them. ***Any other scenario is not acceptable.*** You can do a search for the following to get more information: Trading risk management, money management in day trading, risk of ruin.

If you haven't mastered money management I strongly encourage you to *stay out* of the live markets until you do. To really succeed at trading the financial markets, you need to not only <u>*thoroughly*</u> understand risk reward, position sizing, and risk amount per trade, you also need to consistently execute each of these aspects of money management in combination with a highly effective yet simple to understand trading strategy like price action and supply and demand principles.

The best principle in risk management can be stated in three words. "***Use a stop***"! No one, *especially* a brand new self-directed trader or investor can be prepared enough for the *volatility* and *brutality* of the live market. It is fine to practice on a demo account to learn your software platform for entries and exits however it is completely another thing to be able to do it in a live market environment with the best market participants in the world who are trying to take your money. *Keep it* *simple, be prepared, have a plan and watch your money and you can't go wrong.*

Are you working with a rule based plan yet?

In live market trading it helps to keep the decision making process as consistent and objective as possible. Using a rules based plan for your trading is a *must* and is a trait all successful investors and traders I know possess. A winning plan should be able to sustain your profitability over time in order that you can *keep* all your hard earned profits you make from the markets. Your simple rule based strategy should *only* have you buying at price levels where demand (wholesale prices) exceeds supply and selling at price levels where supply (retail prices) exceeds demand.

The reality of it is that too many undisciplined new traders don't spend enough time composing a rules based plan for the type of trading they wish to do. I have my clients think about what their monetary goals are and then help them compose a great trading plan, becoming a great trader, and attaining their goals.

There is *no room for excuses* in the professional traders mind and thus they know that they are the final decision maker on what is being done or *NOT* done. They are in complete control of all aspects of their trading plan. They have mastered keeping their emotions fully controlled and are aware they are in control of the destiny of there long term investment strategy and management of their portfolio. This is one of the things that make them so successful and it is *all done by following their rule based plan.*

Let me paint a couple of different pictures for you *right up front* so you can get a picture of what it will be like going in the live markets *without* a rule based plan and unprepared or even underprepared in *your* mind. This will give you an idea of what can happen by not having or using a rule based plan in your trading and investing business.

Think of yourself on a nice vacation down in beautiful Australia and you are out sport fishing somewhere around the Great Barrier Reef.

Now you are preparing to set your line but need to get your chum (bait) out first and as you are working on the chum you accidently cut a very deep gash into your leg around your Femoral artery, *and* just at *the* moment you do *that* a rogue wave hits the boat and knocks you *and* the chum bucket overboard and into the water. Now you are the water bleeding profusely *with the chum* and the 21 foot great white sharks that frequent the area you are fishing in. It is said that great white sharks can smell blood in the water for 1000 nautical miles and be in the area in a nanosecond. You can finish this one however *you* like but the sharks win.

The second one is real easy. Imagine you have some huge cajones and you decide you are going play Russian roulette with a loaded revolver that's *fully* loaded. As the song says "click click BOOM"! Only *you* are the one who is going to get FUBAR. That's what you'll be doing by going in the live market unprepared and without a plan. You can kid yourself all you want and say "it will never happen to me" however trust me *it will*.

While these examples may seem harsh to you if you are brand new and have zero experience and are looking for information to get you started in the trading and investing business just remember them when you are screwing around on demo doing all the kooky stuff you *will* do. Demo is where you can do all that crazy stuff you will try, like trading 20 cars on crude oil or gold with no plan. Get it *alllll* out of your system in demo though because the sharks are waiting for you in the live market. The sharks just *might* hand you a loaded revolver so be prepared.

I tell *all* new people I help out that what you will find is that over the course of your learning curve and time in the live markets that you will ultimately find that what is going to work for you and make you money every day or month is a combination of things you have learned over time and have put together to make *your own* winning rule based plan. What works for one trader *will not* work the same way for another however that does not mean you cannot adapt different ideas to fit your own trading style.

Developing a trading plan takes a lot of hard work sometimes as much if not more than actually learning how to trade and operate your platform. It takes time to see what works for you and what does not. It also takes a lot of time to develop the rules that go along with your trading plan. Having a plan and some rules are critical in this business. To not have them and stick to them is a recipe for financial disaster and account ruin.

It doesn't matter how many or how few rules you have in your plan. Most investors and traders I know who are consistently profitable on a daily basis have a simple plan that is perhaps one page or less. It is one thing to have a plan it is however the most important thing to do is to *follow the plan at all costs*. I always say if you are a known rule breaker then just don't too many however you must have *some*.

One exercise I like my clients to do to get them in the habit of following their plan is to pretend they are an airline pilot and they have to follow a checklist at all times and never break any procedural rules or all lives could be lost. Airline pilots by the way are some of the best investors and traders out there in the business today. They are used to doing what I just described and will not deviate for any reason.

Take the last paragraph and just imagine that your account balance is the lives and if you do not follow your plan *all* of your money could be lost. Make no mistake you can perhaps lose *all* of your money by not having and following a plan.

Successful investors and traders know that that having a simple plan is the only way to have a profitable significant *edge* in the live markets. A plan does not have to be complicated to be successful and these consistently profitable investors and traders have come to realize this and actually use the simplest methods in investing and trading which as I said, is supply and demand.

One of the things that traders do is they get monitoring their positions confused with trade management. If you have followed your rules based plan and determined your entry and exit as well as your stop loss and profit target there should be nothing to do really.

What I mean by monitoring your position is to make sure your automated strategy if you are using one is doing what it is supposed to be doing. This is critical as even the best automated strategy can have a discombobulation at some point.

I only recommend using an automated system if you are using it for putting on and taking off positions as well as executing a stop loss and profit target at the same time as the position is being executed in the live market. Then it is truly hands off. All you need to do at that point is to **keep your hands off** the mouse and let the market do all the heavy lifting for you. *Can* you do that?

Until you can monitor your live market positions without actually doing *anything* I strongly recommend that you *stay out* of the real live market with your hard earned real money. Just because you are monitoring what is going on *does not* mean you have to take any action!

The sooner you can get your head around that last statement *the more money* you will be able to make. That's is what you are in this business for so have some control and do what needs to be done to become successful. Be disciplined and don't make the mistakes this book details. Do not become one of the sheeple of the herd and do what everyone else does and study what everyone else studies.

Your job now as a professional investor and trader is to manage your money and control risk at *all* costs. You are basing all of the decisions you make on your developed logic not with emotions. You are confident that you would much rather pursue a low risk entry or have only a small loss if it should happen. It is only low risk, high reward and high probability outcomes that you are looking for now, just like the Wall Street banks and the smart money.

I recommend that if you are not able to give investing and trading your full-time attention, you should have your money managed by someone qualified *who does it for a living*. Learn as much as you can about the trading business, and then when you are ready, you can make the transition to doing it as a full-time business for yourself. You can certainly do the learning and education phase of this business part time however you *absolutely should not do* the trading part of it part time.

Learn to think independently and make *unlimited* money for yourself for the rest of your life!

Your trading method should be what the markets work and that is supply and demand

There will not be anything in this section I will talk about other than supply and demand, and you will find out how to learn how to use these principles in the live markets to make some real money every day. I do not listen to news, I do not use *any* indicators, and there is no fancy system or method you have to learn. It's simple price action, supply and demand, along with training your eyes to see where unfilled smart money orders reside at in the live market. That's it!

Use price action with supply and demand to have a lethal double whammy edge over the sheeple of the herd who have all studied the wrong information from the start on day one, and have been taught unrealistic information that will not help them in any way in the live market. Use price action with supply and demand with sound money management and a detailed trading plan for whatever instruments you desire to work in and there should be no reason you cannot make *some* money every day in the live market once you have studied and prepared yourself properly.

My hope from this part of this book is that you understand how important it is to have a competitive edge when putting your hard earned money at risk in the markets. Each day, the wealth from trader accounts is transferred from those without an edge into the accounts of those who have developed that all needed important winning edge.

The key to success when trading the live markets with supply and demand comes down to a few things: What is the object of supply and demand trading? To gain the ability to objectively quantify bank and institution demand and supply on a price chart, knowing what a supply and demand imbalance looks like and how to take advantage of that opportunity with objective and mechanical rules. Seems simple right?

To be a successful market speculator and investor you must be equipped with the proper tools and information from the start of your trading and investing business. Price action and the use of supply and demand principles to make trading and investment decisions *are* those tools. You don't need to care where the price is going to be ten years from *now*; you need to know about where price is _right_ now.

You don't need any of the latest fad trading systems that the gurus are touting. All you need are the time tested principles of supply and demand. Combine that with the price action of your chosen instrument and you have all the edge you need over the sheeple of the herd.

I purposely do not include any charts, tables, or formulas in this book. No mathematical equations to memorize. I'll tell you why. This book is not about learning any particular method or system. It is about learning how to get the right start on your new business the right way the first time. It is about getting the right information from day one. It is my intent for you the reader to be able to do just that. *READ*.

I would like for you to be able to actually absorb what you are reading as this information will be some of the *most important information you read in your life* when it comes to what you need to know to be successful in the live markets with your hard earned real money. I want nothing but the best outcome for you so I owe it to you to give you best information I can.

OK traders the next place you need to go and the next thing you need to start to grasp is basics and foundation then application of these supply and demand principles in the live markets. You can do a search online for a supply and demand foundation and application course. I encourage you to watch every video and read every article and book you can on this style of investing and trading you can get your hands on.

Here is a good start for you brand new investors and traders looking to understand supply and demand dynamics and use it to invest and trade in the live markets of today. It is economics 101 pretty much. You should learn it though if you want to know and understand what really makes price do what it does in the live market because it is this and nothing else.

So that I do not sound redundant in my explanations after we move on from this point I will direct you to go here: http://www.investopedia.com/university/economics/economics3.asp for an explanation of the dynamics of supply and demand which will from this point be the only thing mentioned as far as a way of investing and trading is concerned in the live market.

Supply and demand is not rocket science and no one owns it, or has a patent on it and *anyone* can learn it. It is a simple market principle that has been in existence since there was a market. It will always be the same principle till there is no more market which will be the end of days.

You do not have to be a math wizard to get it and you do not have to memorize any formulas or math equations. It is just a simple yet powerful principle that when armed with its knowledge and the knowledge of the price action of your chosen instrument of choice you can have a serious winning edge which will give you the highest probability of having a positive outcome on being a market participant.

It all builds off of this basic principle of supply and demand right here so I encourage you to take your time and absorb it a little at a time. You will see that supply and demand investing and trading works on all asset classes on any time frame, it is a robust and repeatable process in *any* market. It does not matter if you are trading equities, Forex futures, grains or *kittens* and *puppies* for that matter. You just have to pick what TF (time frame) you like and what market(s) you want to invest in or trade and what your comfort level of risk is in those markets, it is fairly simple once you have it down pat.

Everything you see on the chart to the left has already taken place hence why all indicators except price action are lagging and of no use to a professional trader. The *ONLY* thing that matters is where those unfilled orders are resting in the market because *THAT* is where PA goes to and takes off from. The only *other* thing that matters is how much time price spent there at that price level. Learn how to read PA in this manner and you will have a high probability of making money every single day. Combine that with supply and demand dynamics and it will be all you ever have to know to make money in the live markets the rest of your natural life.

You do not need to over think *anything* in supply and demand (S&D) trading. It is very simple, the simplest in fact. I had to unlearn 95% of what I had already studied before I became consistently profitable on a daily basis in the markets. My goal is to save you brand new traders and investors who are new and wanting to learn trading a lot of time and cut down your learning curve so you can be on your way to making real money in the live markets every day. How fast you "*get it*" is up to you.

Supply and demand value areas on a price chart represent *ALL* buyers and sellers in the world who are in the live market you are looking at that time and thus it is very easy to quantify were the unfilled orders reside in the live market. As I have stated all you need to do is train your eyes to spot these value areas on the price chart you are analyzing and then make a decision whether you would like to become a market participant as well.

Mostly all of the professional traders I associate with have in the very high thousands of hours of screen time to get good at seeing and opening positions from supply and demand value areas on charts. Hopefully you will get good at it as well and become well off by doing so. The amount of screen time needed to be able to go in the live market and make real money is said to be 10,000 or more hours. Hopefully this book will help get you started and *cut down* that amount of learning curve time.

It is your job to practice to get good at recognizing the value areas. You will need to do it over and over and over again until it becomes second nature for you to spot, quantify and execute a position from these value areas *without hesitation*. As soon as you have learned and have the experience you can open positions from them in the live real markets with real money with confidence and *zero fear*.

What you are looking for is the way PA leaves the certain area which is said to be a supply or demand value area. This value area is also sometimes called a base or PA can be said to be basing. This is that sideways price action I was talking about earlier.

This huge move is normally seen as a large expanded range candle (ERC) or a bunch of them. Does not matter what color you make your candles and I suggest you just have them the same color as the color of the candles will make no difference as to what data the candle is telling you. All that matters is that you understand and become an expert at what to see, quantify it and where it is happening. When PA comes back and revisits this value area again in the future is when you want to be there waiting with your resting order in the live market.

Remember this: first come first served. Which means if your order is already there resting in the live market in the queue you have a high probability of being filled right away verses adding your order and having to wait in line with all the other orders just going in.

The way PA leaves the supply and demand value areas is also the way in tends to return to it. Meaning PA can blast back into the area with a nice big ERC or if it left the value area slowly it can meander its way back. Another way PA can leave a value area is by gapping up or down. What PA is coming back to this value area for is to fill more of the unfilled orders which were left there when price became out of balance the first time it was at this area.

To identify a demand/supply value area: 1. Look at current PA on the chart, 2. Look down and left OR up and left to locate a very strong rally in current PA. Huge candle body's work best or a gap away from it and be an indication of how strong PA is in that value area. Look for the origin of the move, what was the last price the banks were willing to sell at? Is value area fresh? Was there a strong move from this area previously? Draw line on top of basing candle and the lower line on the lowest low of the wicks. The move away from this value area to the furthest point away is the initial profit margin for the next trade op. Move should be 2-3 times the size of the value area for the most profitable trade op. Watch for how far PA penetrates into the value area on the first retracement to the value area. If PA does not quite reach the value area there may be more unfilled orders left at the value area and PA could come back here to fill more orders.

Once PA trades thru a value area and bases (4-6

candles) it becomes a new demand/supply value area. 1st retrace back to this value area is the *highest probability* of a trade working out. 2nd or 3rd retest, and the probability of the trade working out decreases each time PA retests that value area.

Watch for PA to turn on a lower time frame chart at a higher time frame S&D value area, this is the *only* place that a turn in current PA is likely to take place. When trend is changing look at the higher time frame to see *where* the previous value area was and PA should turn there on the lower TF chart. Can also watch for divergence on the indicator *if using one*, it will appear at supply or at demand.

When PA gets to a level that has been touched previously look for an reversal candle such as an engulfing , doji, shooting star with tall wick to the high/low side. Some unfilled orders where perhaps left there and Pa could turn again. After 3 touches watch for PA to trade thru the level and move higher/lower to the next value area. When PA is in a range, oscillators could perhaps be used to go between S&D value areas.

Mistakes traders make in spotting levels: 1. Not quantifying where PA is in regards to the bigger picture TF, 2. Not choosing fresh value areas, 3. Not making sure there is a profit margin to the next opposing value area.

What matters most is that we see where the smart money is deploying their assets and what best pricing they are looking for. We want to get it at what price they get it for. Believe your eyes and not your brains. It's the smart money's ginormous footprints that they leave all over our charts that really matter. It is their tracks in the market that you are looking for on your price chart in the price action of your chosen instrument. They are easy to spot once you know what you are looking for.

Once you are armed with this knowledge it does not matter what you are investing in or trading. These signals I am telling you to see are the only thing that moves price action on a chart. Any chart. Even kittens and puppies if you trade them! If you keep it simple from the start of your learning and education those skills will follow you into the live markets and be beneficial to you in making real money every day.

That's the beauty of it this method. It works on *all* liquid markets and on *any* time frame you choose to look at it on. I encourage you to work on daily charts because that is what the smart money uses. Once you can see the value areas on the daily chart you can see them on any time frame. That's what makes this method so lethal. It's the combination of price action and supply and demand value areas. *That is what wins in today's markets.*

Learn to see unfilled orders on a price chart and the PA of your preferred instrument to trade and you are home. No fancy news, no indicators, just PA and what makes the market do what it does, supply and demand. It's *THE* only thing that makes the market move.

Simple really, however traders tend to make things hard on themselves and cause a lot account pain because of it. Don't be *that* investor or trader. People just think this is a get rich quick business. It's precisely the opposite unless you are a bank or hedge fund and you are using leverage and OPM (other people's money) or a combination of both.

In S&D it's all about setting your position order and then just *waiting* and letting PA come to you. It's just a waiting game at that point. If you get filled there then you are in the market with everything already there. *IF* you do not get filled then you just cancel the order and reassess PA and look for the next signal and opportunity.

The thing about supply and demand style trading is that you either have to be there when PA reaches where you need it to be *OR* have a resting limit order in the market for when it does. That is going to take some getting used to. The whole position order needs to go in at the same time on a trade like that. Stop loss and profit target need to go in with the trade *especially the stop loss.*

If you know how to build out the chart properly you should in fact have an idea where and when PA will get to where you need it be to capitalize on it. You can make big money with the smart money not withstanding HFT's, Algo or AMM. You can't fight that in any way nor should you even try to. Hopefully you are on the right side of it and PA can sail right to your PT on the smart money's volume.

If you are still having trouble seeing the value areas I encourage you to go back and analyze why? Ask yourself these questions. Have you looked back far enough left? Are you using multiple time frames (MTF) to do analysis? Does it help you to understand how to look for and evaluate PA on higher time frame (HTF) charts and how get the curve as well? Look in your journal and analyze what you have done previously that worked and did not. Then just do what *did* work for you over and over and over again!

It is critical that you train your eyes to recognize these areas to acquire your positions from. This is where price is in balance for the moment. The way PA leaves this value area is a key piece of data for you to use in your analysis of any position you may be thinking of taking in the live market with real money. PA will normally leave a value area when it is out of balance with a huge move in PA.

What criteria do you look for when identifying a supply

and demand value area? You're probably asking what makes a supply and demand value area *better* or *worse* than another S&D value area and what criteria is used to determine those issues.? The most important two are how long has time spent at that level and is that level original? How do you define a supply or demand level *before* the fact? Before it is tested or broken through? Look left *as far as you need to* too find out if price has been to that area before. This is the difference between telling if it is a retest of a previous supply/demand level or making a pivot and a support/resistance level.

When does an S&D value area become invalid? An excellent explanation of when a supply or demand level becomes invalid is once PA breaks through and closes above or below the tested level, it is invalid. This is because all orders that were left at that level have been absorbed, thus the candle can close above the value area.

What happens, when a value area is NOT original and PA has been back to it one or more times? Chances are PA will trade through the value area because all of the previous orders that resided there have been filled and/or absorbed. When PA goes to a value area and bounces off 1 or more time orders are being filled and depleted and thus used up so when PA returns back there again it can slice right through the value area and move up/down to the next area of orders.

When PA turns at a value area there will be few candles and low volume, NOT many candles and high volume. Most traders are taught to look for a volume spike and/or many candles and retests of an area for confirmation. By the time they have their confirmation PA has *ALREADY* turned and is moving away and taking the probability of success of a positive outcome on a trade with it, and is also *increasing* the risk.

For me it is all about the value areas. As long I see them right, I make money every day as long as I don't stay long too long. LOL I still draw S&R lines and use TL as well however the trade decisions are based around what PA does at those S&D value areas and if the criteria of the set up meet my rules for entry. If you are more visual then by all means draw some TL or use whatever you like, *do whatever it takes*.

That is how I make money in the live markets every day. I just look for where the smart money have their resting orders and then wait for the retail sheeple of the herd to make their mistakes and buy or sell to or from them and then follow the smart money to where they are going to next. You don't need an MBA degree from a big fancy Ivy League college for that! Combine price action with supply and demand investing and trading and you have an edge over the retail sheeple of the herd.

My hope from this part of this book is that you understand how important it is to have a competitive edge when putting your hard earned money at risk in the markets. Each day, the wealth from trader accounts is transferred from those without an edge into the accounts of those who have developed that all needed important winning edge. *Which one do you want to be?*

The key to success when trading with an edge in the live markets with supply and demand comes down to a few things: What is the object of supply and demand trading? To gain the ability to objectively quantify bank and institution demand and supply on a price chart, knowing what a supply and demand imbalance looks like and how to take advantage of that opportunity with objective and mechanical rules. Seems simple right?

I recommend learning a method of investing and trading that can be used over *all* asset classes and on *any* time frame. The only method I found that does this and works in the live market, because that is what the live markets work on, is supply and demand. I combined that with the price action of the instruments I work in, and it has become a lethal money making combination and what *my* method is based to give me my own winning edge. *Are you ready to get yours?*

The next few chapters will give you some intermediate techniques and principles you can use in your trading to make high profits from the live financial markets. Remember that you must be using *real money to make real money* so using these techniques and principles on demo **will not** work the same way as they do in the real time live markets so you should absolutely be aware of that and be prepared to make them work in your plan to make *real money*.

Having the 3 p's patience, probability and persistence in your favor

The amount of time it takes to learn and become successful in this business is different for everyone. From the very first day when you get interested in investing and trading it can be a *long* road. It can also be *very very* expensive road should you start or continue to make the mistakes detailed in this book.

All of the traders who helped me at the forum I learned at while I was coming up in trading are no longer there. Where did they go? I actually still blog at that forum and try to help out brand new traders who are just coming into the business and have all of the same questions I had when I first got there.

Did those traders who helped me become successful and make a zillion dollars and disappear to their private island with all their market loot? Could be, however I fear that they succumbed to the worst possible thing one can do when they have gone so far in this business. They quit.

I almost did too. They kept me at it though, and answered every single question I had no matter what it was. I can't thank those traders enough for keeping me positive about the whole learning experience. I finally became consistently profitable from staying with it but those traders are not around anymore. I felt bad about it because they helped me so much. That's why I am there answering questions for newbie's when I can. I post as much training info as I can for the new traders to learn from and use to their advantage. One of the training threads I started there has had in excess of twenty five thousand views.

They all told me it would take time, and that is so true. New people wonder how much time will it take them to become consistently profitable. I tell them as long as it takes, there is no rush. I felt I was ready and they did not. The traders at the forum where I was studying and learning, warned me not to go in the live market with real money and that I wasn't ready yet. I was like "I got this"! *NOT*!

I promptly lost two thousand real dollars of very hard earned capital. When I went back for more studies no one said I told you so. Everyone understood and said the same thing. You just need to do more education and study some more. I kept at it and tried a few different methods trying to come up with something that worked for me. That is one thing I tell the traders I help out now. What works for one trader *may not* work for another especially in the live market with real money.

I tell them that what they are going to find is that what is going to work for them in the long run in their own trading business and makes money for them is a combination of things they have learned from others and on their own. They put it all together and all of the sudden they have something going that is making them money on a consistent basis. The *only* thing that matters in the live market is what works for *you* and makes *you* money. Once you have found your edge *never ever* share it!

As has been said many times before investing and trading is not a get rich quick business. It is precisely the opposite, it is a waiting around for the market to pay you type of business. If you can learn to have patience and be decisive you can make a handsome living investing and trading the markets. If you trade Forex just repeat this mantra to yourself: patience means pips and for futures patience means points.

Investing and trading is a business that is all about patience. It is a lot of waiting around for a price to get to where you need it to be to make your money that can take a while sometimes. It requires an iron will not to chase the price or to see something that is just not there. Doing these last two, chasing and seeing things that are not there, will get a new trader into a lot of trouble.

If you are not a patient person or have a gambler's frame of mind, I would say this business is not for you. I was mentoring a trader at the forum I was talking about who was referred to me, and he said he had lost 40,000 real dollars of his savings in the markets. I asked him how old he was, and he said 26. I then asked him how much education he had done, and he replied 6 months. I felt bad for the kid; however, after speaking with him at length, I determined, and he even admitted, that he was a gambler at heart. I wished him well, and that was the end of our relationship.

No amount of mentoring or education I could have provided for this trader would have helped him. He is a gambler, and this business has surely seen them come and go. I have also heard of families finding their loved one with a stool knocked over underneath them in the garage, or the car still turned on. Don't be *that* trader!

As I said, this book is going to be brutally honest about what *not* to do. If you are brand new or have just been in this business for a short time, then this book is for you if you want to make it. The absolute biggest advantage when it comes to being successful in investing and trading, is having stuck with it.

That's when you can feel good and know that no one did it but *you*. The more you try to find the Holy Grail and jump from method to method *the less chance* you will have to succeed in investing and trading, hence the 97% failure rate. Those of us who HAVE made it and ARE successful have traveled a *looooong* road which we now drive our Ferrari's down. Just kidding but you get the point.

Always follow the path of least resistance

The road to consistent profitability and (the front door of your bank) is traveled down the path of least resistance; the smart money shows you the way on the price chart *so why not just let them take the lead down the path?* It is said that it takes 10,000 hours of reading charts to be able to get consistently profitable as a retail trader, why not cut down that time and learn to *let the smart money do all the dirty work.*

Using your charts to know where price turns are going to happen is a function of price and time, and also supply and demand. Study supply and demand trading, and you will have the information you need to make critical decisions required to make money in the live markets with the smart money. They *already know* this valuable information because they are the ones who control the markets.

Do you *need* a crystal ball to tell you what the smart money was going to do? Everyone who invests and trades would like to have one of these, right? Well actually, you do, your crystal ball is your price chart. If you train yourself properly and get the right education and learn the right information from the start, you can use your price chart as a crystal ball to see where price is going to turn before it gets there. You will also be able to predict where it may go to *with a high degree of certainty.*

I have a great idea what price is doing and where price action is going to go before it goes there with a high degree of certainty from quantifying the price action of the asset I am working in. I do this the same way every time without deviation or hesitation. When the chart tells me the information I need to know for entry I act on it with unwavering action according to my rule based plan.

Learning to be a great investor and trader does not have to be a long, hard road—trust me on this. I had to unlearn a lot of things that are of no use to anyone in the live markets. I don't want you make those same errors. Cut down your learning curve so that you can start making *real money* right from the start of your new investing and trading business. Here is a huge tip for you. Always follow the smart money!

This is how I make money in the market today. I sit in the market with a resting order in the vicinity of the smart money and wait for the retail traders to make their mistakes. Then, I watch the smart money pounce on them. It is very easy to spot this once you know what you are looking for on the charts and have trained your eyes to see it at a glance.

The smart money knows the average investors are going to do this, and just herd them to areas where they can be fleeced of their money and then sent on their way. It's just business as usual. Smart money is experts at buying at wholesale prices in the market, and selling at retail. In other words, buying low and selling high. Sounds fairly simple right? The smart money is in the business to make money. Make no mistake about it; they are there to empty the retail investor and traders' account.

Retail investors and traders are the 'sheeple of the herd,' as I said before. They have no idea that they are being led down a one way street that leads to them getting fleeced of all their money. They are the ones who are paying the smart money and losing all of their own assets in the live markets every single day, WHY, because they have been trained to do so.

Once you to start to think like the smart money and adopt their mentality, you can see where they are selling or buying in the live market. Then you can make money right along with them instead of paying them. If you want to be consistently profitable in your investing and trading business, you MUST accept and absorb these basic supply and demand money making principles.

Learning to identify where the smart money is selling and buying on the price chart takes some time. Once you have this skill mastered, you will become consistently profitable almost overnight. Professionals are able to know what the 'sheeple of the herd' are doing even before they do it because they can read a price chart and know where the supply and demand value areas are and where the smart money has their resting orders in the live market. Then they just enter where those orders are and sit back and make money off the smart money's volume.

All I did was study supply and demand trading and train myself to see both of these things happening in the live market. Once I was able to see it at a glance, I immediately started to make money consistently. It took me about a year because I had already studied all the wrong things and had to unlearn about 95% of what I had learned over 4 years. Now I have a double whammy method because I was already using price action.

You must be able to react without hesitation or fear, and have the confidence in your skills to have a resting order in the market where the smart money has their money. You can also use a market order to enter, however you need to have supreme confidence in your skills to do this type of order.

If you bought this book and have zero experience in the markets, I would encourage you as I have said to study supply and demand investing and trading because it is the only method through which markets move from one value area to another. Become an expert at identifying where the smart money has their orders in the live market and then mimic their actions.

Every day part of my morning routine is looking at current price action and looking for where it has already been and could not trade at and *could not stay at* for any amount of time and then I look to where I think the current price action is going to go to with a high degree of certainty. The smart money shows you all this on the chart.

If you know what you are looking for and how and where to look it is honestly not that hard. The smart money leaves clues all over the chart, and it is up to the retail investor and trader to do their homework and spot the smart money's enormous foot prints. Is it possible? *Yes, it absolutely is.*

The smart money cannot hide certain aspects of what they are doing in the market. When the retail investor and trader can read a chart and spot the tracks, they can jump on the smart money's back and let them do all the heavy lifting when the markets shift. Footprints of the big boys are huge, and they paint the picture for you right on your chart every day – *can you see it?*

A consistently profitable investor and trader in today's markets follow the smart money. They take the path of least resistance to reach their goals. Why not follow them and have the way paved for you by their money and their volume. *Just sit back and enjoy the ride.*

3 things that will help you win more trades – large PM, correlation, confluence in signals

Mixing emotions with money-based decisions is usually a plan for disaster! I ask people who come to me for help if they want to be a winner and be right all the time *or be a money maker*. Unfortunately too many brand new traders think that being right is more important than making money. I beg to differ!

Trading success is not just about winning and losing individual trades, it is about making money over time and actually *keeping* it. You must look at the big picture to become successful. It is a common known fact among professional traders that risk/reward ratio, not winning percentage, is the real key to becoming profitable and sustaining a career as a trader for the long term. What seems perfectly logical to do in our minds may not work quite the same in the live market using real money.

I tell brand new traders they must think in terms of probabilities, and get it ingrained into the subconscious of their trading mind. They must be able to ultimately eliminate emotions for every single trade they place. This may perhaps be the most difficult aspect of becoming a true professional trader, but a trait that one simply *must* have to stand any chance of survival—both financially, and psychologically.

Most brand new traders think that they have to win all the time. As someone once said in a movie "thaaaaaths not entirely true"! Being a professional trader means that you actually *will* have some unfavorable outcomes in the market and you are OK with it. I have a positive outcome maybe 40% of the time however I make a double bottom oil tanker full of money from that outcome. The other 60% of the time doesn't cost me a lot, because part of my plan is to know how much I will potentially lose *before* I execute the position.

Should you have a negative outcome on a position if you are using supply and demand it most likely means you saw the value area you opened your position up from wrong that's all, nothing sinister happened. When this happens to me I just know I should have looked further back on the chart to see the supply and demand curve better and perhaps looked at a higher time frame.

If you have followed your plan everything is known *before* you click the mouse to place the position in the market, you know what you are risking as your stop to gain your profit target, all of the information is given to you on the chart. It is your job as the professional to figure out the signals that allow you to identify, quantify and execute quality trading opportunities. Once the opportunity to acquire a position arises you must be decisive and *act without hesitation*. You should *already* have determined what your entry; stop loss and profit target will be *before* executing the position, if it *does not* meet your criteria then just pass and reassess.

It is critically important for you to have the important distinction between indicators (if you are going to use them) that may help you in choosing the right tool to use given the market environment you are trading in. While I am not an advocate of using indicators to trade with, some of them could be beneficial to a trader if they are used properly, and only in certain situations to provide confluence of price action at a supply and demand value area.

Some indicators measure over bought and over sold conditions in a market and some indicate what the trend of a given market is at that time. You should *only* be using the indicators to see these conditions and only be using them as I said, to give you confluence of price action as it is in the a supply and demand value area or approaching one.

This is not to say that indicators and oscillators don't work or that we should not use them. The key point here is that we want to use them in conjunction with price action and supply and demand. Indicators and oscillators are fine confirmation tools when used in the appropriate areas for the right reasons and they are providing confluence of supply and demand value areas and the trade signals you have chosen to use in the plan criteria you've developed.

Make no mistake indicators are *ALL* lagging and only show you what has previously happened. Do you want to make a decision with your real money in real time in the live market with something like that? I sure don't!! Your only goal in trading should be low risk, high probability, and high reward trades, and if you incorporate real support (demand) and resistance (supply) into your analysis you can trade like this and *make money every single day* in the live market just like the banks do.

Always remember that *live market* price action is the *only* indicator that *does not* lag in the information it is providing for you. All the other fancy named indicators do *nothing but* lag in information as they are always late in printing what has actually already happened with price *especially* if you are only trading on a demo account.

Knowing how and when to use *the right tool at the right time* to support your trading decision is critical. Learn the proper way to use your tools and you can make as much money in the live market as you desire. Learn the *wrong way* and you can expect your money train to crash and burn up in those flames and smoke I was talking about earlier and no one wants that now *right*?

Price action is *all you need* to honestly give you all the information you need to make a valid trade execution decision. There is no delay in live price action because it is just that, *live*. If you have a very good software program and an excellent data feed that should be pretty much all you need to give you the information you need to see price action in real time.

All that matters to a professional trader who uses supply and demand principles for their trading are: is the supply and demand value area a quality area and does if offer a significant profit margin. These two things are the *only things* that will make you money in the live market. If you cannot see and quantify supply and demand value areas and use them to base your trading decisions off of, and you cannot determine if you have a profit margin to work with, it is best you *stay out* of the live market until you can.

It is all about putting the probabilities of having a positive outcome in your favor when you are deploying your hard earned capital in the live market. I only enter the market if the chart is telling me that there is a profit margin to be had. All the information is there for you on the chart you just need to train your eyes to see it and *see it in the right place*.

If the data you have analyzed matches up with the criteria in your plan, it is just a matter of being decisive and taking action. I have as part of my plan that my stop loss and profit target all get deployed together at the same time the position is executed in the live market. There is nothing to do at that point but sit back and wait to get paid. Have a winning plan to work in the live markets every day and *you* can sit back and get paid handsomely also.

If the chart data *does not* match up with your plan, and the rules of the plan then there is **nothing** to do. Sometimes the very best action you can take is to take *no action at all*. One of the traits of all professional traders I associate with is that they know when *NOT* to trade. Knowing this will come over time.

How far did price move away from the value area before returning to it? The farther price moves away from a level before returning the *greater* the profit margin and higher the probability of a successful trade. You should only execute a position in the markets only *after* having determined your profit margin and risk.

Your rules should tell you what you are looking for, and you should know *exactly* what your profit target and stop loss will be *before* entry. You can determine this by knowing where the supply and demand areas are on the chart you plan to work on. How far did prices rally up from demand level or down from a supply level before coming back to it? That is the initial profit margin. If you are looking to get 2:1 then the move away from the area should have been 2 times the measurement of the value area or better. This is how you determine your initial profit margin. It will be up to you to decide how much money you are looking to make on any given position. Being conservative can make you a nice living.

Planning out your risk on a position in supply and demand trading is very easy because the chart tells you all the information you need to know. If you want to get 2:1 then you just make sure that the chart of the instrument you are working on is giving you 2:1 or better if you are looking to get 3:1 then look for a profit area that is offering 5:1. This is how you can win more trades if that is what is important to you.

All the information is there for you on the chart. It is up to *you* to quantify and interpret the data and make the decision to enter based on your plan and rules. If the chart you are on *is not* giving you what it is you need then it is best to **not take action**.

Here are some **tips** for using supply and demand to trade stocks (or any other asset class). Look for the way PA leaves a value area on the chart. Also look at *how much time* PA actually spent in a value area. These are two critical pieces of information. You're looking for how much time PA *could not* spend in that particular value area.

Another thing to look for is as I said *how far* PA moved away from the value area before returning to it. This information gives you your profit margin and price target information. Do a search and look up a supply and demand foundation and application course that teaches you this valuable information, they are available online for *free*. Study it hard if you want to be a winner in today's tough markets.

Your rule based plan should include your criteria for entry *and* exit using supply and demand value area information. This information should also have your risk reward criteria as well. If you're set up analysis *does not* give you the correct risk reward that fits your plan criteria then it is up to you to make the decision to not take action, to do so would not be following your plan. This is where a lot of new people make mistakes in the business of trading; they try to see things that *are not there*. It is one of the biggest problems brand new investors and traders need to overcome.

Having a set plan and also having your profit target and stop loss be deployed when your position is executed in the live market is another way to *avoid* making mistakes. By doing it this way, and having a plan you can take out some of the stress involved when your real money is working in the live market. As I always say in every book, the only thing *you* have control of once you are in the live market is how much money you *don't lose*.

In supply and demand investing and trading if you are doing it right, your stop loss and profit target are predetermined before you even take any action. That is the beauty of investing and trading with this method. I encourage you to begin studying supply and demand trading right from the start of your career and the start of your trading business. You will develop an edge that 97% of the sheeple of the herd do not have. This is how you can make money from *them*.

No one can predict what will happen when in the live markets. There are too many things going on all at one time. You *can* however see with a high degree of certainty where the markets will go to if you know *what* to look for and *where* to look for it. If you use supply and demand as your guide in your trading and investing you will know *exactly* what to do.

Here is something to help you put this section in perspective. Banks and institutions *don't use* indicators to base their trading execution decisions on. They also are in the business to make money and not lose it so **they don't day trade**. So if you can get your head around that and then start to think and trade like them and see where they are working at on the price chart there should be no reason you are not making *some* money trading in the live markets when you're ready.

How to overcome over trading as a beginner

There is a line in the song Smugglers Blues by Glen Frye that states "the lure of easy money has a very strong appeal" in trading for brand new traders that is what gets them into a *loooot* of trouble. Don't be *that* trader! The key to consistent profits is not as elusive as most traders think, I ask new traders do you want to get rich *quick* or do you want to get rich *forever*? The easy part of investing and trading is making the mistakes, the hard part is what to do with *all the cash* you will make from being patient and letting the market come to you and give you what you want. What do you like? Do you fancy cars, private jet travel or better yet owning your *own* G650 or perhaps your own little piece of heaven in the Caribbean somewhere?

New people who get into the trading business have dollar signs in their eyes. They are buying Ferrari's and G650's before they ever make a live trade. The unrealistic expectations they have can cloud their judgment as to what is real and not real. All they see is the amount of money that they can potentially make. People want instant gratification and are willing to *do anything* to get it, like taking on large amounts of risk and over trading their accounts; this is especially true of brand new self-directed investors and traders. Unfortunately the markets do not work that way and there are people *already in there* who *do* have a kill everyone mentality and are waiting for brand new investors and traders coming into the business who have the unrealistic expectation that they are different and can beat the market. They know what you're thinking before you *think it* and what you are going to do before you even do it and they're getting rich off of it. Wouldn't you like to be one of *them*?

This section is important for a beginner and will try and get you to think and explain that you don't need to overtrade to make exceptional returns, what you've got to focus on is finding those low risk high-probability trades, they are plentiful if you know *what* to look for *where*. It all builds on those supply and demand principles you studied for your trading method. New traders think that in order to make a lot of money trading you need to take a lot of trades, *which could not be further from the truth*. Over trading is relative depending on the type of trader you are and the time frame(s) used to make trading decisions.

Trading too large for account size and misusing margin and leverage as a beginner are what causes new retail traders to *blow out* their account before they even have a chance to make any money. Brokers make it very easy for you to do this due to the amount of leverage and margin they offer the new trader. They know and are counting on the fact that you have not done much education and you do not have any kind of money management skills.

Overtrading is a problem for a lot of traders who are brand new to the business of making money with money. New traders think they have to be *in there* all the time to be making money and that is simply not the case. They have no idea that they can actually trade less and make more, *much more*. They don't understand or appreciate what you can achieve by going for the only the lowest risk highest reward highest-probability trades; going for fewer trades, but only higher-probability trades.

Many new people coming into this business get in the habit of over trading their accounts from the start on their demo account and they think that they can get away with it in the live market environment. *That could not be further from the truth trust me on that*! A trick I have brand new traders I help out use is to set their demo account balance to whatever amount they think they will be going to capitalize their real money account with, this way they will know *right off* if they can work in the live market with that amount of capital or not.

Most new traders when they hear professionals talking about "over trading" think that over trading is taking too many trades in one day or at one time. Over trading is simply using more margin than you have the account size for on any given trade. The rule of thumb is to only use 2% of your account size as a stop on any one trade. You should start off with this in mind as a beginner and then compose your money management plan for the account size you will be trading and also what asset classes you will be working in.

A huge mistake new investors and traders make is that they come into the business undercapitalized and have not prepared themselves for the circumstances of losing some money. It takes a good amount of beginning capital to start off in the live market in order to give yourself a chance of have a successful outcome to your career and business, and a new investor and trader needs to be well capitalized in order to be able to test out their plan and method if they have developed one. How much money is being well capitalized?

As a general rule of thumb the number most professionals recommend starting with at least twenty five thousand dollars of investing and trading capital to start out for a new investor and trader to be well capitalized in order to be able to test out their plan and method if they have developed one is with for trading full size contracts and positions. This amount of money will enable a new investor and trader to see if they really have what it takes to do this business in a live market environment and have some longevity. I have also seen the numbers as high as 50 to 100 thousand dollars. I know this is *not* what you wanted to hear however I am trying to keep it perspective for you. It is also another reason to read this book *very carefully* and grasp and understand the principles it talks about fully. Unless you are *very very* good and/or very lucky or a combination of both you need to realize that you will surely lose *some* money when you first start out investing and trading real money in the live market, *it is pretty much a given.*

To go into the live market with 2-3 thousand real dollars is *not necessarily unrealistic* as long as you were only using it to trade a micro Forex or micro-cap stocks. To try anything else with that sum of money is not recommended at all. You have to remember to always take into account the expenses of making money with money, it's not free, there is exchange and settlement fee's to be paid along with commissions.

Consistently profitable day traders are the ones who typically take only the few quality opportunities offered to them every day, typically near the open of the trading session. These traders are usually very good at making key decisions on the fly and do well. Day trading also allows traders to take advantage of the many short-term imbalances in the markets each day however you have to have trained yourself to see these imbalances to be able to capitalize on them.

Here is a quick *tip* I can give you. Supply and demand is *most out of balance* at or near the opening of trading in any financial market. This is the best time to be looking to execute a position into the market. Have a resting order at your noted value area and let the market do all the work for you to give you your fill. If you don't know what you are doing, **don't trade at the open**. But if you do trade because that is the time when most of the transfer between accounts occurs, *morning is the golden opportunity.*

The downside of intraday trading is that it is made to look attractive due to the get rich quick aspect of the business. While you can perhaps do very well in a short period of time, 97% end up losing money in this business. There is also the added difficulty of competing with market makers, HFT's, and AMM's at the day trading level. Day trading is the most time-consuming style of trading as it requires you to be in front of your computer screens while you're trading. If you are not good at making quick decisions you are not likely to succeed at day trading. You'll also need a **huge** freakin trading capital account!

I also tell clients just starting out to set their demo account balance to the amount of starting capital they have in mind to work with in the live market when they begin to trade live. I tell them to program their demo account to add in all commissions and exchange fees they will be paying in the real market. As I said there are expenses to making money with money.

This information is easy to get from the broker you will be using. Just ask them what the cost of one round turn will be and also what all exchange and clearing fees would be on that round turn. This information is critical to have in order to have a real world market feel when practicing your skills on demo. Once you have all the numbers just plug them into the demo platform you will be using and then you will have a somewhat accurate picture of what you will be doing in the live market in real time for when you begin to use real money.

Just always keep in mind that investing and trading on demo *is not real time* and the orders you are executing *are not* being transmitted to the live market. There is no one on the other side of the positions you are executing. In the live markets for every seller there has to be a buyer and for every buyer there has to be a seller. The markets only work on supply and demand.

When you are ready to go live with real money I encourage you to start off with a micro Forex account to get yourself familiar with live real money trading and executing live positions into the real time markets. You can start off with a live money micro Forex account for **as little as 500 dollars** depending on what country you are in. Once you have some experience with using real money and the jitters have subsided then perhaps you can move into some other asset classes after you have built up your account to be able to take on more risk.

With real money on the line you must always have your positions planned out *before* ever executing a position order. I recommend to my clients that they have their stop loss and profit target executed with the position order for a no stress *hands off* entry. To do this you need to be utilizing a trading platform which will allow you to build an executable strategy of this type. Do your research to find out which software will allow you to do this.

To actually make a daily living from investing and trading, professionals are trading a large account size in order to be able to trade a sizable amount of contracts known on the inside as trading "size". Most professional traders trading an account size of one hundred thousand dollars or more are seasoned professional investors and traders who have done the time and have successfully built up their account size over a long time to be able to trade enough size to make a living doing trading and investing as a business.

Remember this, leverage kills accounts. If you have to use leverage as a beginner it is best you just *stay out* of the live market until you can enter and be properly funded in your live trading account and if you *are* going to use leverage you had better make damn sure you understand *everything* there is known about using it and what the can happen to you if you get over extended and lose all of your money.

I strongly encourage you to take in what I said in that last paragraph. Should you try to go into the live market unprepared and underfunded you will be doing it of your own volition. Don't say I did not try to give you the right advice here because I am. I will say it one more time *for the sake of your account*. If you try to go into the live market underfunded and under prepared training wise you will LOSE ALL OF YOUR MONEY! Don't be *that* trader!

Chasing trades and trying to *be in* the market all the time and forcing trades out of boredom are a *huge mistake* brand new trader's make, if you are working with a rule based plan for what you are doing in the live market you should not have this problem. Your rule based plan is the only thing that tells you when to take a position or not. If you are following your plan, you should never be over trading and you would never be forcing a trade or seeing something that is not there. I hate to tell you this, but if a setup is not there *it's not there*! Trying to be in the market all the time only leads to over trading and high costs of doing business. Remember there are still costs of day trading and the lower you keep your costs the more money you will have in your account to work with in the market.

In supply and demand trading the chart tells you what to do. If you have trained your eyes to see where the unfilled orders are in the live market you should only be looking to execute positions at those areas and nowhere else. You are only looking to execute a position if the opportunity is telling you that it is a low risk high reward high probability opportunity.

The absolute *best way to avoid over trading* is to have what you consider a trade to be built into your rule based plan and let your plan criteria tell you whether or not you should actually take a position *or not*, this will keep your emotions out of the game. You should have rules for quantifying what you think price action is doing in regard to the bigger picture of supply and demand on your trading chart. If you have these types of rules in your rule based plan to begin with there should be *no reason* for you to be in a position unless the criteria of your plan have been met.

Having a set plan and also having your profit target and stop loss be deployed when your position is executed in the live market is another way to *avoid* over trading and making mistakes, by doing it this way, and also having your plan automated you can take out some of the stress involved when your real money is working in the live market. As I always say in every book, the only thing *you* have control of once you are in the live market *is you* and how much money you *don't lose*.

How to overcome the fear of "pulling the trigger" on a trade

The absolute only way you as a retail sheeple of the herd trader or investor will be able to make a living in the live market on a consistent daily basis is to be 100% confident in your skills and have *zero fear* or apprehension about being decisive when it comes time to pull the trigger on a live trade. The logic, rules, and strategy of S&D trading are certainly not rocket science; however brand new traders tend to complicate things for themselves at the onset of their trading careers. The challenge comes in when you actually attempt to execute a consistently profitable strategy on a regular basis.

When trading properly, you have to get excited to sell after the majority of the sheeple of the herd has bought and after a big rally in price, this will challenge every emotional bone in your body to the core, and can be very daunting for a beginner. This chapter is about some ways to help reduce the emotional obstacles to consistently profitable trading for a brand new beginner.

To make a living as a professional trader, *especially* doing it intraday you will need to be trading a *very large* risk capital account. I *strongly advise* against day trading unless you have a very large capital account and can trade size. What do I mean by a large capital account size? I mean one hundred thousand or more dollars to start. This is really the *only way* you could make any real money by trading intraday and make a living at it.

The one thing I *can* tell you that works, is keeping it simple and it will be. I strictly am a position trader now. I made some money day trading and *got the hell out*. I don't day trade anymore and I don't recommend you do either. I know you won't listen to me at least for now and you will day trade so just learn it the *right way* from the start if that's what you want to do.

So here are some ways that a brand new beginner can reduce the emotional impact of working in the live markets with their hard earned real money. The first way I tell new traders they can do this is by simply making the candle color on the chart they use the same color. Most people use red and green candles which make for a cool looking chart but *may not always* be the best choice for real trading in the live market with real money and I'll tell you why.

If you are selling short *after* a rally in price and *into* an objective supply level (which is the highest probability shorting opportunity), you are likely getting ready to sell short *right after a bunch of big green candles form*. Selling short after a series of big green ERC candles is scary as hell and *not* comfortable as that creates the strong illusion that price is going to keep going higher, *what is even scarier is that it absolutely could*. If you are doing it in gold or crude it could cause you to *piss your pants* if you're wrong!

This huge move is normally seen like I previously have said as a large expanded range candle (ERC) or a bunch of them. Does not matter what color you make your candles and I suggest you just have them the same color, as the color of the candles will *make no difference* as to what data the candle is telling you. The *only* people that can make an ERC in the live market are the smart money. The color of the candles is not nearly as important as the location of the candles the smart money is making.

All that matters is that you understand and become an expert at what to see, quantify it and where it is happening. When PA comes back and revisits this value area again in the future is when you want to be there waiting with your resting order in the live market or be at you're work station ready to click the mouse and execute the position. Here is another **tip**. You already can see where price traded at, you need to see and quantify where price *could not* trade at.

Once you learn to see these value areas and quantify them *in real time* you will be able to invest in any asset class on any time frame, you will also be able to have the confidence to *set it and forget it*. This is the most robust method of investing and trading there is today and has been this way since the beginning of time.

Every new trader thinks they need some magic method or indicator and they are *sadly mistaken.*

Set it and forget it trading is also one of the names for supply and demand trading. In this type of method you can set your resting order in the market based on your rules and analysis and then just *wait for price action to come to you*, doing this can greatly reduce the stress of trying to click the mouse to pull the trigger when it is time to do so.

The investing and trading business is a business that is all about patience. It is a lot of waiting around for a price to get to where you need it to be to make your money and that *can take a while sometimes*. It requires an iron will not to chase the price or to see something that is just not there. Doing these last two, chasing and seeing things that are not there, will get a new trader into a lot of trouble. **IF IT'S NOT THERE, IT'S NOT THERE!** All the more better to only work from a rule based plan that has criteria that tells you when to execute a position.

Only do what you know to be true when working in the live market. The value areas are *quite easy to spot* once you have trained your eye to look at current price action and then look up and left as far back as you need to go. Spot them, draw your lines accordingly, then *wait* for PA to come back and fill your resting order you have waiting. If you are using an automated strategy which as

I said, I *strongly* encourage you to do, all you will have to do is *set it and forget it*, sit back and wait to get paid. When you set and forget it can truly give you all the free time you are looking for from your brand new trading business *and then some*. If you are willing to put forth the effort and learn how to trade with a *set it and forget it* mindset you can have a very nice life from trading the financial markets.

If you are there with your order you can take advantage of this movement and make money from it. I also recommend that you have a stop-loss order and a profit-target-exit order attached to your entry order when it is in the live market waiting for price action to come and fill it. I suggest you automate *as much* of your trading plan as possible and let the market do all of the dirty work for you.

All you have to do when your order is executed is sit back and wait to get paid, very simple, it honestly doesn't really get any easier than that! To be successful you must be able to filter what is *real* and what is *not*. That takes a while to learn, however it is do able. You just have to want to do it. Just ask yourself this one question: do I want to continue to lose money? Your answer should be a no brainer! Smart money shows you the money – can you find it? Open your eyes and smell the money.

I tell newbie's the day you "pull the trigger" and go from your demo account to your real live trading account your whole world is going to change including your emotions. It did for all of us who have made it and it will for you as well. You *will* have to do it (pull the trigger and trade live) however the better prepared you have made yourself for the outcomes the better you will do from the onset of your live market activity. You need to be on point need and at the top of your game when pulling the trigger with your capital, if you are not; you most certainly *can* and *will* get FUBAR.

All traders who have overcome the fear of pulling the trigger on a trade who have become consistently profitable *use a solid uncomplicated rule based plan*. They have achieved their long term success by properly executing their plan flawlessly over and over and over again. They are prepared to execute a position at all times with zero fear or hesitation and this is just one of the traits that make them successful. Make no mistake about it, you better have overcome *any fears* of clicking the mouse to execute a trade and be *completely prepared* to work in the live market before you ever set foot in there with *real money*.

Your rule based plan should be solid by now and include your criteria for entry and exit using supply and demand value area information and any other metrics you have incorporated into your plan. This information should also have your risk reward criteria as well. If you're set up *does not* give you the correct risk reward that fits your plan criteria then it is up to you to make the decision to not take action, you now know when *not* to trade.

I tell new traders they can *be* wrong after they pull the trigger, they just can't *stay wrong*, as it could be will be death to their account! If you have taken a position and it starts to go against you, it is not time to panic and start trying to exit. Why? If you have created a rule based plan that takes into account that a position might pull back a little you will have a protective stop loss there to save anything catastrophic from happening, *right*.

A traders strict adherence to their rule based plan ensures that they have the edge needed to pull the trigger in the live markets every day with *zero fear* and have the confidence in knowing that by following the plan they will be giving themselves the best possible opportunity for a high probability positive outcome and ensuring their long term survival in the live markets.

Your trading plan will be the difference between *success* and *failure* in the live market. When you are writing and making your trading plan you will need to keep in mind what type of trader you have decided on becoming and what your goals will be. Your trading plan should be tailored to the type of investing and trading you will be doing in the live market and also reflect your psychological makeup which will also help when you *do* pull the trigger on a trade.

The plan you make for trading is entirely personal and should not reflect what *any other* investor or trader is doing. How you become successful is going to be entirely dependent on *you* not someone else. You are in control of your investing and trading business and your plan should be your own. Once you have your psychology and emotions under control you will achieve consistency and be able to make as much money in the live markets as you desire. Combine that with solid money management principles and you will have become a professional investor and trader who can pull the trigger on a position and just sit back and enjoy the ride.

There is also a lot of fear involved in trading. When traders make a mistake in their analysis, which causes them to take a loss, they can develop a fear of being wrong all the time. This can psychologically prevent them from "pulling the trigger" when they need to. I remember the first time I pulled the trigger with real money and executed a live market position. My hand was physically shaking after I clicked the mouse and I thought my heart was going to burst out of my chest it was beating so hard. I have a laugh about it now but man that was a *crazzzy* adrenalin rush for sure, it gets easier though, trust me.

Another great way to overcome the fear of pulling the trigger and filter out fear and greed from your trading is to automate it. When you see that your criteria of your rule based plan are set up in the market you should set your resting order in the live market and then let your automated plan do all the work for you.

You should filter out news, events, and all data that *will not* help you in the live market and automating your metrics can also help with this. You now know that the *only thing* that matters in the market is where the imbalance of supply and demand is and where the smart money has their resting orders in the market. Additionally, you must know where the retail 'sheeple of the herd' are making *their* mistakes also.

When smart money is buying *you* want to be buying, when smart money is selling *you* want to be selling. You know *what* they are doing and can see it on your price chart. You are now *investing like* and *trading like* they do and therefore shall make money *with* them all day, every day.

It's this kind of motivation, mental toughness and highly competitive by nature as well as an inner driving force to overcome competition that fuels the best traders to go the extra mile to achieve their goals. Having a "kill everyone" mentality to work in the live markets and pulling the trigger when everyone else *is doing the wrong thing* can be daunting to say the least and will challenge your being to the core. Call it being contrarian or whatever you like but if you can't do it (pull the trigger live) you should just stay the hell out of the live market until you can.

Successful traders know their own trading personality profile, they know what makes them tick (no pun intended again). They all have developed all the personality traits needed to be a consistently profitable market participant over the long term. They develop habit patterns such as having a morning routine that they do religiously every day before trading. This also helps them to be relaxed and to able to just pull the trigger without fear every time, kind of like a machine would.

The take away from this chapter is that you *will* need to be prepared to work in the live markets with your hard earned real money. You can trade and learn your trading platform on demo however you **will** have to pull the trigger and trade live with real money at some point. The choice is entirely yours as to *how* you will prepare yourself psychologically to compete with the best traders and investors on the plant on a daily basis and make money.

A trading checklist can be a subpart of your trading plan or a condensed trading plan, it could even be a type of scoring sheet to check off that you can reference when you're on the edge of your seat about to jump in the market. Your check list should include all the parameters of what you exactly need to execute a trade. If all of the parameters on your checklist *are not met* then your check list *is not* complete and it is good to take no action. Cash is also a position, always remember that.

This checklist is one thing that can really be of assistance to a brand new trader in the sense that they can have something to follow as a guide line that works in conjunction with their rules based trading plan they have composed for the type of trading and investing they wish to do.

What does a check list need to have on it you may be asking? Your trading check list is going to be the most personal part of your plan actually because it is going to tell you whether to pull the trigger *or not* to execute a position in the live market with real money. Should your parameters not be met on the check list, as I said in the last section, it is going to be best to *take no action*.

Something your check list *could* include as basics are: What is the trend is it up or down. Is it approaching a supply or demand value area? If you are using any indicators are they giving you buy or sell signals in that supply or demand value area? Are there any important data points coming out that could be a catalyst for price action to be pushed into your charted supply or demand value area? Are there any of your indicators which are giving you confluence for trade execution? Are there any of your candlestick reversal signals in the value area?

These are just some basics that can be on the check list. You will need to do *a lot* of searching within yourself to develop what your execution signals will ultimately be though. No one is going to be pushing the button on the mouse *but you* so it is important to have it all down pat *before* you push any buttons.

When it all started to come together for me it was not until I start using the principles of supply and demand in conjunction with price action that I started to really see a change in my profits. I had to go back and learn the basics of what supply and demand are to be able to understand how to utilize them in the live market. Supply and demand is the *only thing* that moves price in the market.

Now I can place a resting order in the live market, get driven to the airport, board a plane a fly anywhere on the planet with confidence and zero fear. I truly set and forget. Stops are in; emotion *is out* as it were.

The thing I count on knowing is that my stop loss and profit targets are in the live market as well. There is *nothing but time* at this point which has enabled me to write this book you are reading and all the others I have out currently. When you do a set it and forget it trade *you had better have done your homework!*

One more great way that can help you to pull the trigger on a live trade and to really succeed at trading the financial markets, is for you to thoroughly understand risk reward, position sizing, and risk amount per trade, you also need to consistently execute each of these aspects of money management in combination with a highly effective yet simple to understand trading strategy like price action and supply and demand principles. As a brand new beginner people *do not do this* and it ends up costing them *some* or *all* of their hard earned money in the beginning and it doesn't have too.

Concentrate on having on a solid well-constructed trading risk plan. The better your plan is, the more you're going to be able to move forward with confidence and zero fear and be able to pull the trigger without hesitation. You can also identify when your best trading schedule is. When do you find you do your best trading, during RTH, Asian session, London? If you can determine what time works *best for you* it can greatly help with your profitability. Only go in the live market you work in when the liquidity providers are providing liquidity in your market.

The consistently profitable trader is actually *very excited* about pulling the trigger on a trade because they know that the trading opportunity is very low risk, as you are entering your position as close to your protective buy stop as possible *and* it is all automated so you can be *truly hands off*. Make sure you always *adjust your position size* to a level that you're more than comfortable with and when it's time for entry, instead of watching the chart and fearing a potential loss, focus on *how low risk the opportunity is*. I'll say this one more damn time. *Only trade with capital that is disposable so if it is all lost in the markets there is no emotional attachment to it.*

The best traders *are the best* because they constantly try to improve themselves. I can't stress enough how important this mindset is in trading. The markets are dynamic, and they will demand the very best of you *day in and day out*. Automate your plan, keep your losses small, use mono colored candles then just set it and forget it. Pull the trigger, make money!

Here is a trick I give the people I mentor to use. You want to get the best price in the market right? Buy low sell high as it were. Cut out a coupon (any coupon) out of the paper and tape it to the top of your trading station monitor so you can always see it. Then when it is time for you to pull the trigger look at that coupon and ask yourself "am I really buying low" "am I really selling high"? After a while you will have broken yourself of any bad habits, trust me.

Only two things can happen, you can be paying **them** every day or you can be making some money right along with them. Don't be the one who pays be the one who *gets* paid!

Ways beginners can increase their winning percentage for higher profits

I always ask brand new traders who come to me for help if being right all the time, winning lots of trades or making a lot of money is the most important thing to them and then I wait for their answer. The answer I always get is "I want to make money", hell we all want to make money in the financial markets it is what they are there for.

Unfortunately, new traders think that winning trades is more important than making money, **IT'S NOT**. Nothing is more important in the live market than making money! Dig this, you can be wrong 40-50% of the time and still make a double bottom oil tanker full of money. You can be wrong, you just can't *stay* wrong. Winning and being right are typically things that brand new people to the business associate with being profitable and successful, that could not further from the truth.

Your entry needs to be correct in trading the live markets, meaning low-risk, high-reward, and high probability, if it is not, the other components of your trade, such as the exit and management will not work in the manner they should. This section focuses on some simple and powerful methods related to how you *can* and *should* increase your winning percentage as a beginner so you can make money *right away*. First and foremost though, you must have a full risk and money management plan in place in your overall trading plan for any of the following ideas to work. You *must* have a complete handle on what your own appetite for risk is and what your trading capital account can allow you to trade with.

*W*ays beginners can increase their winning percentage *right away* are always make sure they have the correct *profit margin* that meets their plan criteria for what a profit margin is to them. That can *only be determined* by you as to how much you want to make on a given position. Your profit margin from your value area is the distance from your entry to your profit target.

*A*n S&D value area is a price level where there is competition to buy or sell an instrument. If you are trying to buy where others are looking to buy, you are going to have to compete with them at that value area which makes getting filled there challenging for a beginner trader. A much *easier way* to get your buy/sell order filled, is to buy/sell *before* price reaches the value area where there is *less competition* to buy/sell and gives you a much *easier* and *better* chance at getting filled. Another way to think about it is instead of buying when there is competition to buy/sell, buy/sell back for your profit when there is still competition to sell/buy.

*S*o here you go then. If you are looking for trading opportunities that offer you 3:1 risk reward, make sure the chart is offering you at least 4:1. If you are looking for 4:1 risk reward, make sure the chart is offering you at least 5:1. If you want to increase your winning percentage *even more*, if you are looking for 3:1, make sure the chart is offering 5:1 and take profit at 3:1-4.5:1.

You must be able to qualify and quantify real demand and supply in *any* and *all* markets with a very high degree of certainty. There is *no guessing* to this, either you know how to do it or you don't. If *you don't,* take some advice here and *stay the hell out of the live market* until you have it down pat and can execute positions without hesitation and know what you're looking for as far as your PM. The smart money gives you *all the information* you need to do this, and is clearly seen on a price chart if you know *what* you're looking for.

The next way to up your winning trades is to *only trade from original value areas*. What does that mean you're asking? To only trade form an original value area means to only initiate positions from a value area that has *never been tested* once it became a value area, hence being original. This is the *only time* and place you want to be executing a position from and also the only place where the smart money will be working from. If you have learned how to spot them and quantify PA on a chart you should have no problems identifying an original level. Did you look up, left and back far enough? That is one mistake brand new trades make in identifying original value areas, they don't look back far enough on the chart to make sure the area they are looking at is not just a pivot area.

Another way to increase your win percentage is with an important edge-building consistency tool which is to use a "smart plan".

The consistently profitable winning professional investor and trader *only* enters a position based on their plan which normally calls for the stop loss and profit target to be *already known* before the position is even entered. I personally use an automated entry so there is *no emotion in it*. I just set the entry parameter in the live market and when I am filled everything is done for me. All I need do at that point is wait to get paid. There is zero stress, zero drama, and zero complications.

There is no letting a position that is in profit come back to turn into a loser due to having the stop loss already in the live market. I have entered the position *already knowing* what my stop loss amount is money wise so there is *no question* as to how much I will lose should the position not work out as planned. Once the profit target is hit the position automatically closes and then it is time to look for the next opportunity.

Most of these professionals have what I call "smart plans" meaning their position is managed from the time it is executed in the live market until the time it closes itself out at the designated profit target. Notice I said closes *itself* out. That is because most professionals including me use an automated system to do their trading.

My smart system executes my trade and places the stop loss and profit target right when the trade is executed. There is no doing anything manually. Once the position is executed it either makes money or gives me a small but manageable loss. Most of the time, I don't even look at the chart and am not even there while the trade is working. I am at the beach, or the cigar club or anywhere but in front of the chart, that is the beauty of the smart plan, it's smart.

Having a "smart plan" should be the goal of *every* trading business. Smart money management should be a part of every trading strategy and it is something that I really stress all the time to new traders who come to me for help. I tell them to just *stay out* of the live market until they have a plan composed that they know works for them that is suited for their personality type and also the type trading which they desire to do.

New traders make the mistake of not having a plan to manage their trade once they get a fill and once that happens *they have no idea how to deal with it*. They sometimes get panicked when the trade is suddenly making money and they don't know what to do to manage the equity they have in the position and will close the position prematurely.

The best way to filter out fear and greed from your trading is to automate it. When you see your criteria of your rule based plan is set up in the market you should set your resting order in the live market and then your automated smart plan *do all the work for you*. The chart tells you *what to do* and *where to do it* you just have to have a solid plan for what to do with the information the chart gives you. I even have a smart plan for long term horizon positions I am in. The smart plan automatically moves up the SL when the PA of the existing position moves up a certain amount, the entire management of the position from open to close is *hands off*.

Another way to enhance the information you can get from supply and demand value areas on the price chart you are working is to use multiple time frame analysis (MTF). You can also use MTF analysis to line up a smaller TF value area with a larger TF value area from the big picture that is happening in the market you are working in. Using multiple time frames is a must for being in the right place at the right time on a price chart. Use MTF to stack the probabilities in your favor and up your winning percentage at the same time. I only look at daily charts to trade from so my HTF charts are the weekly and the monthly. Sometimes if I need to see historical data I will search out a 30 year chart online. You can look at some historical charts and get data at http://www.macrotrends.net/

Should you have a negative outcome on a position if you are using supply and demand it most likely means you saw the value area you opened your position up from wrong that's all, nothing sinister happened. When this happens to me I just know I should have looked further back on the chart to see the supply and demand curve better and perhaps looked at a higher time frame. You need to always be aware of the big picture. Using multiple time frame (MTF) analysis or correlative charts is the way to be aware of what is happening in the big picture and I will be discussing that in just a little bit.

If you are still having trouble seeing the value areas I encourage you to go back and analyze why? Ask yourself these questions. Have you looked back far enough left? Are you using multiple time frames (MTF) to do analysis? Does it help you to understand how to look for and evaluate PA on higher time frame (HTF) charts and how get the curve as well? Look in your journal and analyze what you have done previously that worked and did not. Then just do what *did* work for you over and over and over again!

Also using correlative markets can be an advantage for a new trader's win percentage. How I use correlative markets is to see when one market is up the reverse should be true in the other market. The ones I do this with the most is the VIX and the S&P. I love to trade the ETF VTI which is a total stock market index fund that mirrors the S&P's PA. I know then when the VIX is going down the S&P is going to go up. VTI will go up/down right along with the S&P because it has the same PA patterns and value areas. Only work from the right value areas you have marked off on the charts you work from and you should be able to make money right along with the smart money.

One problem that arises when a trader gets good at seeing the value areas is that when they mark them off and put their resting order in the live market what happens is that their order does not get filled. It is because the banks and hedge funds are working there. Your 1 lot is *going to have to wait* until the banks 100 thousand lot order is filled. You can always try to front run them, just remember that if you do you will be *increasing your risk* and might be going off your plan if the front running parameter is not built into your plan.

The last way to have a good win percentage is to have a thorough understanding of probability boosters and how to *use them to your advantage* to give you a winning edge over the competition you have in the live markets which is as I have said, the smart money, Wall Street banks, hedge and mutual funds and *alllllll* of the other professional traders around the world who "*get it*" and work off of a rule based plan they have composed for their style of investing and trading.

Probability boosters are different parameters that can help clarify whether you will want to execute a position or *not* in the live market. They are called different names in the trading business I just happen to use this particular moniker. They all do the same thing and give the same result provided they are learned the right way and used properly.

All professional investors and traders I know are prepared *before* they step foot in the live markets and know there is no such thing as winning every single time, *it's just not realistic*. They know before they enter a position what their odds are of having a positive outcome. They have stacked probability in their favor and have the confidence to be in there competing against the best investors and traders on the planet. They do this with probability boosters.

Use probability boosters as a way to increase your winning edge, when using them in conjunction with your supply and demand trading. These probability boosters can help you to increase your chances of gaining a low risk high reward high probability entry in the market *which is all you should be looking for* when deploying your capital into the live markets. Another name for these probability boosters is odds enhancers or probability enhancers although it is just semantics as they all have the same function in your rule based trading plan.

While there are quite a few of the probability boosters you can study and utilize in your trading and investing. I will give you the four main ones now in this book then you can go out and do a search online for the rest of them and then pick which ones you may want to use and incorporate into the rule based plan you will be using to trade with.

The four biggest probability boosters are: 1. how much time did price spend at a value area? 2. How fast did price move away from the value area? 3. How far did price move away from the value area before returning to it? 4. Has price action ever been back to that area yet? Number 3 is also the probability booster that provides the information about your profit margin.

There are a lot of other ways and extra things like probability boosters to aid the trader in the use of supply and demand that are beyond the scope of this *basic* book. I will have another book coming up soon that details how to use probability boosters to see more trade set ups so be looking for that book soon at all of your favorite booksellers online. Remember, probability boosters are parameters you can use in your trading plan to give an extra edge over your competition to *put the odds in your favor* in the live market and increase your winning edge.

When you have mastered your trading strategy and combined that with the money management principles in your money management plan, it will only be a matter of time before you are making consistent profits in the markets and winning as much as you want.

A competitive edge includes as I said earlier a mental edge with discipline, laser focus, and a fail-proof strategy. Enforcing some rules in your strategy is critical and following them *at all costs* will absolutely make sure you can beat the competition. I always say that if you are a known rule breaker, then just don't establish *too many*. However, the ones you *do* have must be followed as if your very life depended on them, as I said, *your account balance certainly does*!

Trading in today's markets is competition at the very top level, where the stakes are the highest. Educate yourself to be a competitor and a winner. You want to have success, right? You need to do it right then!

Front running the smart money

The highest probability setups come when price comes back to smart money values areas to fill more unfilled orders of the smart money. This is the time you want to have your order resting in the market just before the area so you can get filled. This is commonly called *front running* and is how you as a retail trader will have to do it at these areas if you want to get filled. *Why* do you have to do it this way, competition that's why! If you think that you are going to be able to put your 1 lot or 1 contract order in an area where the smart money is looking to fill an order of perhaps 200 thousand, *you would not be thinking realistically.*

The chart of what you are looking at gives you all of the information you need. It is up to you to read the information and quantify it then make your decision. You are only looking to execute a position when you can have your stop loss as close to your entry as possible. This is the only way the smart money does it and how you should as well if you want to make money with the smart money on a daily basis if you desire to day trade. I do not encourage you to day trade however if you must you need to have all the probabilities of having a positive outcome in your favor, *the smart money certainly does.*

What makes a high probability setup you may be asking? What criteria are needed for a high probability setup? Well that is really up to *you* and how you have it set up in your rule based trading plan you work from for whatever instrument you are working in the market. *You do have a rules based plan don't you?*

Successful traders are only looking to enter trades that offer the lowest risk highest reward and have the highest probability of having a positive outcome. They do this every day using supply and demand trading. It does not matter what instrument you are trading or what time frame you are doing it on. Supply and demand is the *only way* the live market works. For every buyer there *has* to be a seller and for every seller there *has* to be a buyer. It ***can't*** work any other way.

The price chart you are looking at tells you all the information you need to know to make a decision to execute a position *or not*. If there is no value area to work from, then hey guess what, *there is nowhere to work from* and you should <u>stay the hell</u> out of the live market until there is.

The most difficult part of supply and demand trading is the waiting around for price to get into your value area you have charted. You must develop the patience to *just sit and wait* for the market to give you what you want. It will when it is ready and until that time you need to sit on your hands and **resist** the mouse. Can you hear Tom Petty singing "the waaaiting is the hardest parrrrt", now you will! LOL

The market is a game. The competition is of universal proportions. The novice retail investor or trader has an enormous handicap. They often aren't even aware they are playing a game; let alone what the rules are. The smart money are the makers of the market, hence the deciders of the rules in the *live* market, and it is as I said, competition at the **absolute highest level**. Why, because it involves money. You had better be *well-prepared* and *well-funded* to compete with the top traders in the world. Like I said, if you think that you are going to get your one lot filled at a supply and demand value area before the smart money *I have news for you*.

You are not only competing with the smart money at supply and demand value areas on the chart for entry. You are also competing against *all the other professional traders in the entire world* who "get it." The live market is competition at the universal level as I have said, and it is *imperative* that you be well armed to battle against the best people in the world.

The smart money moves the market with all their money. However, it is all the other people who you are competing with for entry that you have to be prepared for. One way you can increase your chances of beating them is to place your order in the market before they do. By 'front running' as it is called, the smart money and the other competition, you can gain entry before them and get paid by everyone who enters after you.

This includes the smart money if you should, by some chance, beat them to a fill.

How *do* you front run the smart money? Well, you already know where the supply and demand value areas are on the chart, so with that information in mind you can then map out your entry, stop loss and exit plan and place your order in the live market just a few pips or ticks in front of where the actual value area begins, that's it really, however **the further out you front run the more you <u>increase your risk exposure</u> so always be aware of that**.

Front running is a more advanced technique and you better **be sure** of your skills before you try it. They are looking at the very same market you are looking at and seeing all of the same information. How everyone interprets this information is what makes traders so different. That is why it is vital to have a trading plan that is tailored to *your style* of trading for the asset class you desire to work in.

There is also actually another *very easy way* to beat them to a fill and *make them do what you want* before they take PA to the value area. You can just click the mouse and buy/sell at market and *make* them fill you. How do you *make them* fill you may be asking? The answer is very simple and I already said it above. All you have to do is press the button and you're in, *BOOM*. Then what? You better damn sure have your SL pre planned and your exit if you trade in that manner all mapped out. Live action is not going to wait for you to figure it out. I have a NT ATM strategy that enters all orders at the click of the mouse upon entry. No fumbling around at all.

You are now asking what about slippage? I liken slippage to paying the cover at the strip club, you want to see titties *right*? You pay the $20 cover or whatever it is, **BOOM** you see the titties. In the live market if you want to make money with the big boys and use a market order to do so, you pay the cover, slippage. Remember they are the Wall Street banks and all the rest of the biggest players in the world you are messing with in that area. They can stay at a price level *waaaaaay* longer than your account can remain solvent *so remember that*. For me, it's about seeing *where* they are, and trading *with* them not against them, *try it and you will surely get* FUBAR!!

One problem that arises when a trader gets good at seeing the value areas is that when they mark them off and put their resting order in the live market what happens is that their order does not get filled. It is because the banks and hedge funds are working there. Your 1 lot is *going to have to wait* until the banks 100 thousand lot order is filled. You can always try to front run them like I have said in this section, just remember that if you do as I said, you will be *increasing your risk* and might be going off your plan if the front running parameter is not built into your plan.

What is high probability trading?

Successful professional traders are only looking to enter trades that offer the lowest risk highest reward and have the highest probability of having a positive outcome. They do this every day using supply and demand trading. It *does not matter* what you are trading or what time frame you are doing it on, supply and demand is the *only way* the live market works. For every buyer there *has* to be a seller and for every seller there *has* to be a buyer, it *can't* work any other way.

Keep that last sentence in mind if you are brand new and you are just demo trading right now to get the feel of your software, there *has* to be someone on the other side of your trade to give it to you when working in real time so what you're doing on demo *may not work the same way* in the live market working against the best traders in the world live and in real time.

The price chart you are looking at tells you *all the information* you need to know to make a decision to execute a position *or not*. If there is no value area to work from, then hey guess what, *there is nowhere to work from* and you should <u>stay the hell out</u> of the live market *until there is*.

The most difficult part of supply and demand trading is the waiting around for price to get into your value area you have charted. You must develop the patience to just sit and wait for the market to give you what you want. It will when it is ready and until that time you need to sit on your hands and *resist* the mouse. Can you hear Tom Petty in your ear right now singing "the waiting is the hardest part", now you will!

The highest probability setups come when price comes back to these values areas to fill more unfilled orders of the smart money. This is the time you want to have your order resting in the market just before the area so you can get filled. This is commonly called front running and is how you as a retail trader will have to do it at these areas if you want to get filled. Why do you have to do it this way, competition that's why! If you think that you are going to be able to put your 1 lot or 1 contract order in an area where the smart money is looking to fill an order of perhaps 20 thousand you would not be thinking realistically.

The chart of what you are looking at gives you all of the information you need. It is up to you to read the information and quantify it then make your decision according to you rules. You are only looking to execute a position when you can have your stop loss as close to your entry as possible. This is the only way the smart money does it and how you should as well if you want to make money with the smart money on a daily basis if you desire to day trade. I do not encourage you to day trade however if you must you need to have all the probabilities of having a positive outcome in your favor, *the smart money certainly does.*

What makes a high probability setup you may be asking? What criteria are needed for a high probability setup? Well that is really up to *you* and how you have it set up in your rule based trading plan you work from for whatever instrument you are working in the market. *You do have a rules based plan don't you?* There are some probability boosters that you can use to give you an idea of how to put the probabilities of having a position outcome on your position in your favor. Let's talk about those next.

In supply and demand trading it is all about putting the probabilities in your favor. *All* you should be looking for are low risk high reward high probability entries on the chart you are working on. Another way to enhance the information you can get from supply and demand value areas on the price chart you are working is to use multiple time frame analysis (MTF). I encourage you to study MTF if you are going trade in the live market with real money.

How to put the probabilities to make high profits in your favor – using probability boosters

Advanced price action analysis can be very beneficial to traders provided they are looking for the *right type* of information to help them. In supply and demand trading there are several ways to see price action in an advanced manner. There are some things called *probability boosters* that can help you determine the validity of these areas and also help you to quantify them as well. I will be discussing those probability boosters shortly.

Probability boosters are different parameters that can help clarify whether you will want to execute a position or *not* in the live market according to your rule based plan. Probability boosters are called different names in the trading business I just happen to use this particular moniker. They all do the same thing and give the same result provided they are learned the right way and used properly.

Probability boosters as I call them are parameters you can use to put as I said above the probabilities of having a positive outcome on a position in your favor every time you go in the live market. They are called other monikers by other people however they all mean the same thing and provide the same information. You are looking to use this information to make a trade decision based on your rules for trading whatever it is you trade or invest in. If you are not using a rule based plan to trade I strongly encourage you to stay out of the live market until you have one.

The most important thing you need to remember in learning supply and demand trading is that price on a chart shows you what has *already* happened and where it happened from. What is important to you is not where price traded at but where price *could not* trade at. When price was trading at this value area it could not stay there for any period of time, why? Once you can see this picture of imbalance of price you can begin to quantify and make trading decisions from the information you get from your price charts.

All professional investors and traders I know are prepared *before* they step foot in the live markets and know there is no such thing as winning every single time, *it's just not realistic.* They know before they enter a position what their odds are of having a positive outcome. They have stacked probability in their favor and have the confidence to be in there competing against the best investors and traders on the planet. They do this with probability boosters which help them to be proactive about a possible position.

The smart money leaves huge tracks in the market when they move price with their power and money. They can't hide this footprint they leave and it is your job to track them and then do what they are doing where they are doing it from. The probability boosters help you track the smart money's movements and then take advantage of the way smart money moves price to the next value area.

While there are quite a few of the probability boosters you can study and utilize in your trading and investing. I will give you the four main ones now in this book then you can go out and do a search online for the rest of them and then pick which ones you may want to use and incorporate into the rule based plan you will be using to trade with.

Here are the 4 main probability boosters I use in my trading. There are others however these are the ones I use every single time I execute a position in the live market. I never trade without them. The four biggest probability boosters are: How much time did price spend at a value area? How fast did price move away from the value area? How far did price move away from the value area before returning to it? Has price action ever been back to that area yet? Next let's talk about some *basic* information on what to look for and how to use the information you get from the probability boosters to enhance your having a positive outcome as a live market participant.

How much time did price spend at a value area? The less time spends at a level, the more out of balance supply and demand is at the level. Most significant and key turns in price will happen here, and there will be very few candles and/or little volume. The more out of balance supply and demand is the less trading activity there will be at the level. The less time PA spends at the level the more out of balance S&D is at the level, look for 3-8 candles this is the most ideal and volume will be low here.

What you are looking for is the way PA leaves the certain area which is said to be a supply or demand value area. This value area is also sometimes called a base or PA can be said to be basing. It is critical that you train your eyes to recognize these areas to acquire your positions from. This is where price is in balance for the moment. The way PA leaves this value area is a key piece of data for you to use in your analysis of any position you may be thinking of taking in the live market with real money. PA will normally leave a value area when it is out of balance with a huge move in PA.

How fast did price move away from the value area? What you are looking for is the way PA leaves the certain area which is said to be a supply or demand value area. How did it move away from the area, was it gradually or an explosive gap? Gap is best and indicates huge imbalance. Explosive is next best and then gradually. Price will come back to the area in same manner it left normally. The stronger the move away from a level the more out of balance S&D is at the level. When the last order is filled at the value area and there are no more buyers or sellers, price must leave the area.

This huge move is normally seen as a large expanded range candle (ERC) or a bunch of them. Does not matter what color you make your candles and I suggest you just have them the same color as the color of the candles will make no difference as to what data the candle is telling you. The *only* people that can make an ERC in the live market are the smart money. When you see a huge ERC in the live market with a lot of volume in it they are the one's making that happen.

All that matters is that you understand and become an expert at what to see, quantify it and where it is happening. When PA comes back and revisits this value area again in the future is when you want to be there waiting with your resting order in the live market. Here is another tip. You already can see where price traded at. You need to see and quantify where price *could not* trade at.

How far did price move away from the value area before returning to it? The farther price moves away from a level before returning the greater the profit margin and higher the probability of a successful trade. You should only execute a position in the markets only after having determined your profit margin and risk.

You should know exactly what your profit target and stop loss will be *before* entry. You can determine this by knowing where the supply and demand areas are on the chart you plan to work on. How far did prices rally up from demand level or down from a supply level before coming back to it. That is the initial profit margin.

Your rules should tell you what you are looking for. If you are looking to get 2:1 then the move away from the area should have been 2 times the measurement of the area or better. This is how you determine your initial profit margin. It will be up to *you* to decide how much money you are looking to make on any given position. Being conservative can make you a nice living.

Has price action ever been back to that area yet? The more original the area is the higher probability that price will return to that area. Why, because there are more unfilled orders left there that did not get executed from when PA was there previously. The first time PA comes back to this original value area is the best and highest probability chance of having a positive outcome on a position. How far does PA go back into the value area once it returns for the first time? The further it goes in the more orders are used up at that level. Once PA goes 25% into the value area stop taking it.

After the first time PA comes back to the value area your odds of having a positive outcome start becoming diminished. There is no need to execute another position from this area again if you have already had a positive outcome and made some money. Don't get greedy!

Professionals always employ a rule based method of using a stop loss and will sometimes exit a position even before their stop loss is triggered if they feel their analysis was in error even if it means taking a small loss on the position. They are fully aware that if their money is deployed in the market in a losing position they are not able to use it for something that could be making them money. They have no problems with exiting to be able to re-assess and they know that the next thousand trades are coming right up.

Experienced investors and traders know when to enter. They don't chase the market and let price come to them to give them what they need and let the market do all of the dirty work for them. They are successful because they know they don't have to take every set up and that they can afford to miss out on something that would have perhaps had a positive outcome for them and they know that there will be plenty more opportunities coming right up.

They only are looking for set ups which offer a low risk high reward outcome that has the highest probability of success for them. Professionals only execute a position that that has a stop loss which is as close to their entry as possible to have the lowest amount of risk on the position and consider this a most critical part of their risk management plan. They are aware of how they will do this even *before* they execute a trade. They also know what their profit margin is as well as their margin of error before taking a position also. The probability boosters give an extra edge.

I use an automatic entry method with my own investing and trading which has my stop loss and profit targets executed right along with the position going into the live market. I might have a positive outcome on only 40-50% of my positions however the amount of profit I realize from the best outcomes far outweighs any negative out comes. Many of the most successful investors and traders I associate with are wrong way more than they are right about the markets. They just employ sound money management tactics that keep them in the game making money every day and also use the probability boosters as part of their rules based plan.

They know that there *will* be some losses and they are part of doing business and also learning. Experienced professionals know what is involved with having an edge in the market, how to employ it and make it work successfully to make profit. They will always turn a negative into a positive. I strongly encourage you to study probability boosters to add to your trading strategies and entry strategies.

There are plenty of chart examples and more probability boosters and how to use them at the link I posted above which I will post again here for your convenience.

http://www.forexfactory.com/showthread.php?t=428204. Don't worry that the thread mostly is dealing with Forex trading. The idea is to learn all the rules and to lean to see supply and demand in real time. All of the rules of using supply and demand for your trading are listed on the first page of this thread. I encourage you to print them out and study them thoroughly then begin looking at the chart examples the traders there have posted.

Once you have learned all the rules and are able to see and quantify supply and demand in real time and can combine that with the price action of whatever instrument you desire to work in you will have a double edged sword that can make you as much money as you would like to make in your trading business.

Experienced investors and traders know when to enter. They don't chase the market and let price come to them to give them what they need and let the market do all of the dirty work for them. They are successful because they know they don't have to take every set up and that they can afford to miss out on something that would have perhaps had a positive outcome for them.

They only are looking for set ups which offer a *low risk high reward* outcome that has the highest probability of success for them. Professionals only execute a position that that has a stop loss which is as close to their entry as possible to have the lowest amount of risk on the position and consider this a most critical part of their risk management plan. They are aware of how they will do this even *before* they execute a trade. They also know what their profit margin is as well as their margin of error before taking a position also. There are some probability boosters that can give an extra edge in determining your profit margin and I will talk about those shortly.

Another way to enhance the information you can get from supply and demand value areas on the price chart you are working is to use multiple time frame analysis (MTF). There is some valuable information in the bonus section of this book that may help you in composing your rule based plan that deals with the time frames you can work on using supply and demand in your investing and trading.

Why you need to always look at the bigger picture

Another way to enhance the information you can get from supply and demand value areas on the price chart you are working is to use multiple time frame analysis (MTF). You can also use MTF analysis to line up a smaller TF value area with a larger TF value area from the big picture that is happening in the market you are working in. Here is something for you to always remember, higher time frame trading equals higher probability of having success long term *and making more money*, if you are in this business to make high profits this is one of the ways to do it.

Using multiple time frame (MTF) analysis or correlative charts (or both) is the way to be aware of what is happening in the big picture. As a self-directed trader you must always make sure you are trading with the dominant trend and not approaching a major supply or demand value area. Should you have a negative outcome on a position if you are using supply and demand it most likely means you saw the value area you opened your position up from wrong that's all, nothing sinister happened. When this happens to me I just know I should have looked further back on the chart to see the supply and demand curve better and perhaps looked at a higher time frame, you need to *always be aware* of the big picture.

Price *only* turns in trends at a higher time frame value area where orders are still unfilled so you have to be able to see these areas at a glance on your price chart and be ready to take action if your analysis meets all the criteria of the rules of your trading plan. If price is nearing a larger time frame supply value area, then taking trades on the long side has increased risk and diminished the probability of having a positive outcome on a position, conversely the same is true when approaching a demand value area from the larger time frame. Keep in mind that the further away from the value area PA goes once the trend has turned the more your risk is increasing and there is less of a probability of making money on the position.

You must *never* enter a position *after* the trend has turned and a new trend has begun. By entering after the new trend has already begun *you are entering late* and exponentially increasing your risk at the same time. You always want to enter at the beginning of the trend or as close to it as possible and have everyone *who enters after you pay you*, that's the whole idea of trend trading right there. Using MTF can help you to see where the trend will potentially turn with a high degree of certainty once you train your eyes to see the smart money value areas.

The professionals are only interested in making money and doing it by taking a longer term view. The smart money *does not* day trade. They have billion dollar super computers and code slinging geeks making a cool million a year for doing nothing but writing computer algorithms to tell the computer what to do and trust me when I say; they can see *you* coming a mile away. As I said, if you are in this business to make money then you need to see where the smart money is working so you can take advantage of their volume and money power.

It is *imperative* then that since you as a retail investor or trader have a look at higher time frame charts even if you are trading intraday which as I have said the smart money *does not do*. That should be a huge clue, however because people think this is a get rich quick business when they first get into it and they think that they can learn a few chart patterns and some price action and then can go into the live make and make jet fuel money. New traders are buying Ferrari's and Gulfstream 650's before ever making a live trade with real money.

You as a retail trader should be using MTF (multiple time frame analysis) and need to be looking at a minimum of 2 time frames to get your information from and while MTF is a more advanced technique you as a self-directed retail trader *must* put all of the odds and probabilities in your favor with whatever means you can, *smart money certainly does*. The smart money is using daily weekly and monthly charts because as I said, they are in the business to make money long term. They have nothing but a long term perspective and time horizon. Price and time are the best money making techniques there are!

Using multiple time frames is a *must* for being in the right place at the right time on a price chart. Use MTF to stack the probabilities in your favor and up your winning percentage at the same time. I use a daily chart to enter so my HTF charts are the weekly and the monthly to see the curve and see where the huge supply and demand value areas are at. Sometimes if I need to see historical data I will search out a 30 year chart online. You can look at some historical charts and get data at http://www.macrotrends.net/ The supply and demand value areas are where the smart money works from and where I have said you need to be to see on the chart. You need to be able to see these areas, quantify what is going on there and then take action.

To do MTF analysis when working on a daily chart TF you can use the weekly and monthly chart TF for the bigger picture curve. You can also look for confluence signals from candle sticks and any indicators *you* may choose to use. While I *do not* suggest using indicators, they should *only be used* to confirm confluence signals and *nothing else* as most indicators are only printing data *after* it has happened. The only true non lagging indicator is pure price action which is happening in real time right before your very eyes. If price moves up, demand exceeded supply/longs shorts and vice versa, the more a demand/supply value area is tested the weaker it gets, because orders are being consumed.

If you should decide that you want to intraday trade good luck with it and at the minimum you should use a daily chart for your curve to see the bigger picture and then maybe a 30 minute for smaller supply and demand value areas to trade from and then a five minute chart for entries. A good rule of thumb according to Dr. Alexander Elder to use a higher TF chart that is an increment of 2, 4, or 6 higher than your entry chart i.e. a 5 minute chart x 6 would be a 30 minute chart for the bigger picture etc. I *do not* recommend you go below a 5 minute chart for intraday trading, and *honestly*, you shouldn't be day trading *at all* as a beginner. Don't say I haven't tried to warn you.

If you are still having trouble seeing the value areas I encourage you to go back and analyze why? Ask yourself these questions. Have you looked back far enough left? Are you using multiple time frames (MTF) to do analysis? Does it help you to understand how to look for and evaluate PA on higher time frame (HTF) charts and how get the curve as well? Look in your Journal and analyze what you have done previously that worked and did not. Then just do what *did* work for you over and over and over again!

All I can say here is that if you really want to *dial it in* and are looking to make money from trading you should be using daily charts and looking at the weekly or monthly charts for the bigger picture curve for the smart money value areas, then you can be there with your resting order and be first to get filled when your risk is the least and your probabilities are the highest of getting paid by everyone who enters after you and is *late to the party*. If you are swing trading, you will know with a high degree of certainty where your profit target can be once you have deployed your capital.

In supply and demand trading it is all about putting the probabilities in your favor. *All* you should be looking for are *low risk high reward high probability* entries on the chart you are working on. If it's not there, **IT'S NOT THERE**! I encourage you to study MTF if you are going trade in the live market with real money.

If you are going to intraday trade you had *better damn sure have done your education and training* and have your rule based plan and strategy *down pat* before going into the live markets with your hard earned real money in real time with the best market participants in the world.

The old buy low and sell high routine

This term is funny because everyone says it however not very many retail traders actually know what it really means or how to do it. Making money in the financial markets today is really *no different* than how you make money in real life. An everyday example is when you go to the grocery store with a coupon to give you a discount on the product you desire to purchase. It's really no different in the financial market; you want to buy something on sale and get the best price you can. Buy low, sell high.

Everyone likes to get a deal right? You go to your favorite Coney restaurant and sometimes have a coupon you cut out of the paper for something on the menu that they are giving a deal on that day. Investing and trading is no different. You want to buy your instrument at the *best possible price* and sell it for the highest possible profit. Hence buying at wholesale and selling at retail. You also want to take the least amount of risk to do so.

We instinctively want to get the most value for our dollar. Why then, would you want to buy when an instrument price is at its highest point in the live market? This is what retail investors and traders do every day. They wait and wait, then before they know it the price has had a big run up and they place an order out of anxiousness, Oopsy!

The problem is that retail investors and traders are conditioned to do just the opposite of this rule. They like *to think* they can buy low and sell high, however they have learned all of the *wrong information* which tells them to do the wrong thing from trading books and/or seminars. The books, seminars, and training that retail investors and traders put themselves through are often *totally unrealistic in real world markets*. Unfortunately, this often goes unrealized until it is *too late* most of the time.

Retail investors and traders buy and sell at the worst possible moments. When the price of an instrument has had a huge move up in price the retail trader is buying at the top of the move. When the price of something has had a huge move down in price they are selling at the very bottom. They have been taught to do this from the start and *don't know any better*.

Unfortunately 97% of the sheeple of the herd retail investors and traders are conditioned in their training to do just this. Here is an example that will hopefully solidify this concept for you so you will never make this mistake above.

This mistake happens in everyday life as well. When you walk into Sam's Club thinking that you are buying at wholesale prices, are you? Do you *really think* that Sam's is selling to you, the retail buyer, what they bought at wholesale? That big screen TV you bought from Sam at the 'bargain' wholesale price of $1200 cost the store $600 because he bought 100,000 of them. You could never afford to buy that way. Sam bought low and is selling to you at higher prices than the items were purchased for, thus, making a tidy profit from you. The same thing happens in the markets every day to the retail trader.

Smart money is total and complete experts at buying at wholesale prices in the market, and selling at retail. In other words, buying low and selling high. Sounds fairly simple right? The smart money is *tooooootally* in the business to make money, which is most of the time *yours* FYI. Make no mistake about it; they are there to empty the retail investor and traders' account.

Retail investors and traders are the 'sheeple of the herd,' as I said before. They have no idea that they are being led down a one way street that leads to them getting fleeced. They are the ones who are paying the smart money and the professional traders thus losing all of their own assets in the live markets every single day. WHY? Because they have been trained and conditioned to do so right from the very start of their time in the business by learning to buy high and sell low.

When learning the business of investing and trading. Retail investors and traders are taught unrealistic principles from the start. They are shown how to buy when what they should be doing is selling and vice versa. They are taught to buy an instrument when all the 'conditions' say it's the right time. Retail traders come rely on indicators which supposedly are to help them make trading decisions. Trust me, no kind of edge or high profits can come from using lagging indicators, no edge = no profits.

Unfortunately for them, the markets operate in precisely the opposite manner. Typically, they are buying at the wrong time when the price is peaking already, so they are actually buying high and after everyone else has already bought and have no one to buy behind them to pay them. They normally do this where supply outweighs demand, so price *must* go down. It is at these value areas where the smart money and professional traders are waiting to take the other side of the retail trader's *mistake trade*. Buy waiting and buying high you have no one to pay *you*. By buying low everyone else who buys *after* you pays you. As I always say, don't be the one who pays be the one who *gets paid*!

Once you to start to think like the smart money and adopt their mentality and you can see where they are selling or buying in the live market, then you can make money right along with them instead of paying them. If you want to be consistently profitable in your investing and trading business, you *must* accept and absorb these basic supply and demand principles *immediately*.

Learning to identify where the smart money is selling and buying on the price chart takes some time. Once you have this skill mastered, you will turn your trading around, I know I did. I had to unlearn 95% of what I had learned over the course of 5 years. However, once I learned this new skill and started investing and trading with this understanding, I became consistently profitable almost overnight. Now I laugh all the way to the bank right along with the smart money. I have honestly become one of those sharks we were talking about earlier.

If you bought this book and have *zero* experience in the markets, I would encourage you study supply and demand investing and trading right from the start of your time in this business because it is the *only method* through which a markets price moves from one value area to another. Look up supply and demand trading online at the clickable link in the extra links section at the end of the book and then watch and learn everything you possibly can about it. Become an expert at identifying where the smart money has their orders in the live market and then mimic their actions. Pretty soon, you will be laughing all the way to the bank as well.

Here is a trick I give the people I mentor to use. You want to get the best price in the market right? Buy low sell high as it were. Cut out a coupon (any coupon) out of the paper and tape it to the top of your trading station monitor so you can always see it. Then when it is time for you to pull the trigger look at that coupon and ask yourself "am I really buying low" "am I really selling high"? After a while you will have broken yourself of *any* bad habits, trust me.

My final advice to new self-directed traders

The reality of the market is that there are people in there who are smarter than you, have *waaaaaaaay* more money than you, have better algo than you and are trying to take your money and transfer it from your account to theirs. They don't know you, care about you, or have any feelings if you lose. It's just business. The business of making money with money and it is always *your* money. Don't be *that* trader. Learn to do this business the right way from the beginning and you won't be.

Don't become one of the sheeple of the herd and do what everyone else is doing when and where they are doing it. The smart money can see this on the chart just like the sharks in the water that can smell blood and are looking to take advantage of the errors the sheeple of the herd make over and over again.

Who are the sheeple of the herd and who are the smart money you may be asking? The smart money is the Wall Street Banks, institutions, hedge funds, HFT's and dark pools. They are the liquidity providers and market makers. They are whom you need to be able to see on a price chart if you want to make money in the markets.

The sheeple of the herd as I call them are the unprepared or underprepared retail traders who are in the market without the proper training and education or psychological makeup who get FUBAR (fleeced up beyond account recovery) every day in the live markets. You also need to be able to see *them* on a price chart because you can also make money from *them* as well.

There are no shortcuts to success in investing and trading. You either *get it* or you don't. You will need to develop a "kill everyone" mentality as I said to work in the live markets on a daily basis to be consistently profitable. You have to do the learning time and have your head on straight if you want to drive the money train.

Only do what you know to be true when working in the live market. The value areas are quite easy to spot once you have trained your eye to look at current price action and then look up and left. Spot them, draw your lines accordingly, then *wait* for PA to come back and fill your resting order you have waiting. If you are using an automated strategy which I *strongly* encourage you to do, all you will have to do is set it and forget it, sit back and wait to get paid. Finally the best advice I can give you is, **always** use a stop and **keep your hand off** that damn mouse!!

There are no short cuts and what I just said to study and learn as far as some of the intermediate techniques and principles can take quite a while. It all depends on you and how much time and effort you are willing to put in to learn what needs to be known to be a successful market participant. When you are learning and think you can skip something because it is boring you to learn it just think about your barbeque and those sharks looking for blood waiting for you in the live market to come in unprepared and without a rule based plan.

The best advice I can give you is *not to enter* the live market with real money until you are ready. It's really that simple. No one is making you do this business. You are the boss and in control of what you are doing, *so have some*. Entering the live market and using real money before you are fully ready and confident enough to do so will only cause you to lose money and question your skills.

You should *already* have all the skills needed to be successful in the live markets *before* you enter. The people who are already in there are professionals who are ready to take advantage of new traders and take all their money. Don't be one of the sheeple of the herd.

It is not rocket science or neurosurgery being done in there. It is making money with money. Usually it is the smart money making their money with *your* money. Is that what you want? Do you want to keep making the same mistakes over and over again and paying the smart money and professional traders who *do get it*?

Trading in today's financial markets it is competition at the very top level, where the stakes are the highest. Educate yourself to be a competitor and a winner. You want to have success, right? You need to be prepared to work with the best market participants in the world. That's who are in there in the live Forex, futures and stock markets.

It is one thing to have a plan and practice it on demo it is however entirely another to execute it flawlessly in the live markets with your hard earned real money against the best market participants on the planet. Trading is global so make no mistake and think you are in there by yourself.

Having a plan and sticking to it is one thing that all investors and traders *must* overcome to be a successful market participant for a long term financial benefit. This should be the goal of anyone considering a business or career in the investing and trading business. Making *some* money every day should be the goal of all investors and traders no matter what asset class you are working in. This is easier said than done though.

Finally it is all about being organized and disciplined. Successful traders have this down pat. They have developed their trading edge over time and have mastered it and built their trading plan around this edge. Some of these traders even go as far as writing their plan out on paper and keeping it with them at all times.

It takes a lot of time and patience to develop this system and these investors and traders have taken the appropriate amount of time to get it down which in turn has made them into consistently profitable and successful market participants.

Learn to use the techniques detailed in this short book and you can become a consistently profitable market participant in no time. It takes a lot of hard work however if you are committed to doing this business then the amount of time it takes is not an issue. The market is always going to be there waiting for you. *ALWAYS!*

To really succeed at trading the financial markets, you need to not only *thoroughly* understand risk reward, position sizing, and risk amount per trade, you also need to consistently execute each of these aspects of money management in combination with a highly effective yet simple to understand trading strategy like price action and supply and demand principles.

Once you learn the core principles of how to trade with supply and demand you will rarely need to go back to reinforce anything. Everything is there for you right on the price chart in front of you. Once you have learned to quantify price action on a chart and then use that information to enter a position in the live market you will not need any other information.

Most futures traders spend many many hours looking for that magical combination of indicators that will reveal the "Holy grail" of winning trading strategies. They should *instead* be spending their time on learning what makes the market actually work which is supply and demand.

Concentrate on having on a solid well-constructed trading plan. The better your plan is, the more you're going to be able to move forward with confidence and zero fear.

Identify when your best trading schedule is. When do you find you do your best trading is it during RTH, Asian session, London? If you can determine what time works best for you it can greatly help with your profitability. Only go in the live market you work in when the liquidity providers are providing liquidity.

The best traders *are the best* because they constantly try to improve themselves. I can't stress enough how important this mindset is in trading. The markets are dynamic, and they will demand the very best of you day in and day out.

There is really no easy way to do it honestly. There is a certain progression of steps *all* new traders must go through to be able to drive their own money train to the bank on a daily basis which I have detailed in the book. The progression of steps is to learn money management, gain a hold on your own psychology, learn to read the price charts of the instruments you choose to work in and finally learn how to quantify real supply and demand in the live market to make your trade decisions from.

As I said, there are **no short cuts** and what I just said to study and learn can take quite a while. It all depends on *you* and how much time and effort you are willing to put in to learn what needs to be known to be a successful market participant. For me it was days, nights, weekends and even some holidays. I just wanted to do it *that* bad. It takes a lot of dedication and time.

When you think you are going to try to shortcut it just remember there are sharks that are looking for your life blood and hard earned capital in the live market waiting for you to take that shortcut so they can take all your money.

Remember in this business your account can get burned beyond recognition and recovery so remember the smoke and flames coming out of your barbeque because you threw all your money in there and didn't have a rule based plan as to how to work in the live markets where you are in competition with sharks.

Brand new traders tend to self-sabotage their own efforts at the beginning of their trading careers and businesses because they had not learned that there is a lot to know and have mastered before one can become successful in this business. There are a lot of different things we can do to improve our trading, but there are also things we can do to sabotage our trading as well. One of those things is not getting or having enough information.

It is my goal in this book to give you the information that can help you right from the start of your new trading business the first day. It is so important for traders to start out right from the beginning because the outcome of not having done so is very expensive and no one likes to or wants to lose money. Unfortunately brand new investors and traders tend to lose almost all of their money on their first try in the markets.

I recommend you start off slow and build on success. You should study each part of what those new beginner series books talk about in detail separately and *master* each individual process before moving on to the next one. How long will that take? As long as it takes! There is no reason to be in any hurry because the market is there waiting to pay you some money every day.

I like to think of it as a big ATM machine because it is open virtually 24 hours a day seven days a week just about. You just need to have the proper PIN# to get your money out. Do the training and education and do not make these mistakes in this book and you will be well on your way to having your own personal PIN# to make money in the live markets every day. It is all about putting all the probabilities in your favor to attain the lowest risk highest reward highest probability outcomes you can have in the live market when putting you hard earned money to work on a daily basis.

Oh and by the way. That big screen TV you paid the $1200 for at Sam's he bought for $600 marked it up and sold it to you for a tidy profit. When you are getting ready to execute that position in the live market think about the TV and ask yourself am I really buying at wholesale?

Extra links
http://www.informedtrades.com/index.php has a huge amount of free courses for the brand new investor and trader.

This is a great *free* supply and demand learning thread http://www.forexfactory.com/showthread.php?t=428204

Here is a link to a video that teaches how to draw the proper type of lines around a supply and demand value area.
https://www.youtube.com/watch?v=jRjdR_kPMyw

Much more information on Forex Futures can be found on the CME website, The CME is: www.cmegroup.com.

You can look at some historical charts and get data at http://www.macrotrends.net/

Here is a great link with a lot of frequently asked questions by brand new traders and investors. http://education.howthemarketworks.com/stocks/beginner/practice-stock-trading-questions/ I encourage you to have a look and try to absorb a little bit of the basic information at a time. You don't need to know it all by heart verbatim however it can help you to understand some of the mechanics of how the markets work.

This link helps you to have a better understanding of how stocks are affected by supply and demand.
http://www.investopedia.com/university/stocks/stocks4.asp

The next links will really peel your eyes open and make you think if you really want to get into this business or not. All links provided in this section are working as of the writing of this book.

https://en.wikipedia.org/wiki/Fractional-reserve_banking

https://www.youtube.com/watch?v=TcGldf0UFXU this video is long and I suggest you watch it in 30 minute segments and then try to digest the data. It's scary because some of things the presenter is talking about happened in 2008 and he is talking about them in what I would guess by the clothing and cars is the 1980's. 2008 financial crisis had not even happened yet.

This next video will only compliment the one just above and you should watch it and pay strict attention to some of the things the people being interviewed are saying.

https://www.youtube.com/watch?v=z7nTplUffXg

I encourage you to share these last two videos with everyone you know and love.

Glossary
Glossary of terms and abbreviations

ATM = automated trade management

AMM = Automated Market Makers

AI/AO - All in all out

Base or basing = an area where price is moving sideways and price is in balance.

BP = Big or bigger picture

BO = break out

DD = Due diligence

EOD = End of day

EOT = End of trend

ERC = Expanded range candle

FUBAR = fleeced up beyond account recovery

HH = Higher High

HL = lower high

LL = lower low

LH = lower high

HFT = High frequency traders

IMO = in my opinion

IPO = Initial Public Offering

S&D = Supply and demand

SM = Smart money - banks, large institutions, hedge funds etc.

TMI = to much information

MTF = multiple time frame analysis

PT = profit target

SL = stop loss

FOMO = fear of missing out

TC = Trend confirmation

ONL = overnight low

ONH = overnight high

OB = over bought

OS = over sold

PA = Price action

PM = Profit margin

PDL = previous day's low

PDH = previous day's high

SPEC = speculator

S&R = support and resistance

Range bound = sideways price action

TF = time frame

Trending = PA is in an up or down trend

ROI = Return on investment

RTH = Regular trading hours

TA = Technical analysis

TL = trend line(s)

TOS = Think or Swim

VAP = value area proximity

Disclaimer

This book is for educational purposes only. Futures, options, equities, and spot currency trading have large potential risk and traders should be well-educated before putting real money at risk. You *must* be aware of the risks and willing to accept them in order to invest in all markets. *Never trade with money you can't afford to lose.* This book is neither a recommendation or solicitation, nor an offer to buy/sell a futures contract or currency.

Forex, futures, stock, and options trading *are not* appropriate for everyone. There is a substantial risk of loss associated with trading these markets. Losses *can* and *will* occur. *No* system or methodology *has ever* been developed that can guarantee profits or ensure freedom from losses. *No* representation or implication is being made that using the trading concepts methodology or system or the information in this book will generate profits or ensure freedom from losses.

HYPOTHETICAL OR SIMULATED PERFORMANCE RESULTS HAVE CERTAIN LIMITATIONS. UNLIKE AN ACTUAL PERFORMANCE RECORD, **SIMULATED RESULTS DO NOT REPRESENT ACTUAL TRADING**. ALSO, SINCE THE TRADES HAVE NOT BEEN EXECUTED, THE RESULTS MAY HAVE UNDER-OR-OVER COMPENSATED FOR THE IMPACT, IF ANY, OF CERTAIN MARKET FACTORS, SUCH AS LACK OF LIQUIDITY. SIMULATED TRADING PROGRAMS IN GENERAL ARE ALSO SUBJECT TO THE

FACT THAT THEY ARE DESIGNED WITH THE BENEFIT OF HINDSIGHT. NO REPRESENTATION IS BEING MADE THAT ANY ACCOUNT WILL OR IS LIKELY TO ACHIEVE PROFIT OR LOSSES SIMILAR TO THOSE SHOWN.

www.ingramcontent.com/pod-product-compliance
Lightning Source LLC
Chambersburg PA
CBHW071436180526
45170CB00001B/366